UNVEILING SECRETS FROM EDEN'S GARDEN

DR. ETIENNE M. GRAVES JR.

PUBLISHED *by* PARABLES

Earthly Stories with a Heavenly Meaning

Unveiling Secrets From Eden's Garden

Dr. Etienne M. Graves Jr.

PUBLISHED *by* PARABLES

Earthly Stories with a Heavenly Meaning

Books Coming Soon..

"Did You Get The M.E.M.O.?"
Melchizedek's Excellent Ministry Order

And
Dawn of a New E.R.A.
Exciting Realm of Angels

Written By
Dr. Etienne M. Graves Jr.
M.E.M.O. (Melchizedek's Excellent Ministry Order}
P.O. Box 4505, Ontario, Ca, 91761
etmelchizedek@yahoo.com
@UnveilingSecrets
@etiennememo

Table Of Contents

DR. ETIENNE M. GRAVES JR.

INTRODUCTION

Almost 20 years ago I had a dream from the Lord, that took me until now to understand. I saw people walking in the darkness in a trance and under a spell. The whole world was under this spell. It was covered in Darkness. People were walking like zombies towards the edge of the earth. As I watched this from a distance, I screamed out to them to turn around and go back, but they could not hear or see me. One night some years ago, I woke up in the middle of the night and on my television was a cartoon, *"Family Guy,"* and it was showing the 1960's television sitcom, *"Bewitched."* Samantha crashed into the moon and died as she was riding her broom. Then the screen went black and it flashed the words, *It Was Witches!* I then heard a loud voice say, *"IT'S TIME YOU KNEW THE TRUTH!"*

The Lord began revealing the truth to me. The truth about what was really going on. He showed me that we are living in a false reality and it began in the Garden of Eden. If you ask someone what happened in the Garden of Eden, they will most likely tell you it is about a snake, Adam, and Eve, and how they ate an apple from the forbidden tree. But that's simply not true. What you are about to learn is, that is not what happened. In fact, you will be surprised when you see what really happened in the garden.

DNA, sex, magic, witchcraft, Occultism, Freemasonry,

False religions, and much, much more, all had its origination in the Garden of Eden. This book will pull back the curtain and unveil the secrets that are in operation today from the garden. It is because of the lies and false identity that Lucifer is able to keep the church in bondage. You can't win a battle if the people that you are warring against, are in disguise, and their methodical attack against you is camouflaged. The truth will set you free. The Lord disperses revelation only at His appointed time. Now is that time, and these are the days.

So, fasten your seatbelt, grab a chair, some popcorn and your KJV Bible and enjoy this book. It is stranger than science fiction, and more fantastic than anything you can imagine. It is more fantastic than any fantasy that you have seen or read. Because it is true. So, without further ado, from The Holy Ghost, M.E.M.O. Ministries, and D.N.A. Productions; I present to you and I will be...............
"Unveiling Secrets from Eden's Garden."

"It is the glory of God to ***conceal*** *(keep secret, cover by hiding)* a **thing:** But the ***honour*** *(splendor, glory)* of kings is to *search (examine intimately)* out the matter." (KJV) - *Proverbs 25:2*

1. DNA:
God's Signature of Life

There are many secrets and intricacies that God has hidden and woven into His Holy Word. There are also secrets and secret places that only God, angels and demons know about. This book is full of these secrets. Many of these secrets have not been revealed because it was either not the appointed time to be revealed, or no one has done the research to dig out the secrets.

According to Amos 3:7, *"Surely the Lord God will do nothing, but He revealeth His secretsunto His servants the prophets."* One of these secrets is that DNA is the blueprint to our *"Book of Life."* Our DNA or *"Book of Life,"* is written to determine exactly who we are. Anything that has life has DNA, or a book. Our unique DNA is the blueprint for our personal *"Book of Life."*

In Psalms 139: 13-16, *"For what hast possessed my reins: thou hast covered me in my mother's womb. I will praise thee; for I am fearfully (and) wonderfully made: marvelous (are) Thy works; and that my soul knoweth right well. My substance was not hid from Thee, when I was made in secret, (and) curiously wrought in the lowest parts of the earth. Thine eyes did see my substance yet being unperfect; and in Thy book all my members were (to determine what DNA does) written, which in continuance were fashioned, when as yet there were not of them."*

Our DNA was made before we were ever born on the Earth. God took our DNA (our substance) and filed it on the shelf under our name where it stayed until it was transferred into His Book of Life when we receive Jesus as our Lord and Savior. David explains the correlation between books, writings, and DNA in this verse. DNA sequences can be read like a book.

The Greek word for book is *biblion* or *(biblos),* and is where we get the word, *"Bible."* It means a roll, book, scroll, writing, or a bark scroll, or bark of papyrus plant. The original word of God was written on scrolls. It is significant because Deoxyribonucleic acid or DNA looks like rolled up scrolls or a spiral ladder. It consists of two strands that twist or make helical turns in a circular motion. The word *ribo* in deoxy*ribo*nucleic acid, comes from the Hebrew word, *"chalav."* It is related to gum and the Hebrew word, *"gome."*

Gome is the source of papyrus paper and the Bible. This all connects to the Word, and the Bible. In the Bible, *universe* means one verse, word, sentence or line. Also notice the word *adverse* in *adversary* which is Satan. Satan wants to add or to take away verses from our DNA since we are as He (Jesus) is, and the Word. His words are spirit and life according to John 6:63. When we are trying to reach the destiny He has planned for us and live the Christian life according to the Bible (the Word of God), the *"world,"* gets in the way. Satan who is a liar puts the "world' in our face instead. Satan is trying to keep us from the Word by putting in the letter *"l"* in the word. Righteousness and dominion are two of the benefits of salvation for those who have Jesus' DNA. Because of Jesus righteousness, we have dominion. The "l" in world stands for liar, which is in between the *"r"* and *"d."* Our righteousness and dominion is what we receive when we walk in line with God's word, and not listen to Satan the liar.

In the Bible there are many secret keys, codes, or hidden words that can and do relate directly to DNA because of its spiral, circular shape and twisting motion. Some of these words are: *whirlwind, twist, spit, turn, circle, cycle, wreathe, weave, twine, roll, scroll, book, ladder, stairs, staircase, vines, vineyard, ivy, life, seed, generations, blood, bloodline, born, birth, birthright, family, womb, secret, members, water, tree, plant, man, woman, children, animal, wife, marriage, flesh, cleave, side, body, flesh, stones, tabernacle, temple, cross, grass,cover, veil, amber, bdellium, and gold.* Some of these terms, will be explained later, but for now, let's focus on the words: spiral, twisting, and circle.

The Earth, sun, moon, stars, and planets are all shaped like a circle (despite the false flat earth theory), and they have a DNA. The only time the word circle is mentioned in the KJV Bible is in Isaiah 40:22, *"It is He that sitteth upon the circle (circuit, cycle, to describe, revolve), and the inhabitants thereof are as grasshoppers; That stretcheth out the heavens as a curtain, and spreadeth it out as a tent to dwell in."* Let's break down this meaning. A circuit makes a circle.

As for the word circuit, we know that electricity must have a circuit for it to work. That is how a battery works. It takes a positive and a negative electric current that causes a chemical reaction to complete its circuit. A battery has two ends; a positive terminal and a negative terminal. When two terminals connect to a wire, a circuit is formed. Electrons will flow through the wire and a current of electricity is produced. Inside the battery a reaction between chemicals take place. Batteries convert chemical energy into electrical energy and continues a cycle throughout the life time of the battery.

Concerning the word cycle, we know that seasons, days, months, and years move in cycles. Everything in nature moves in cycles, that is why they call it the, *"cycles of nature."* One of the definitions for circle is to describe.

The human DNA tells our body what to do and who we are, in a way to identify or describe us. It describes our genetic make-up (hair color, eye color, height, etc.). The meaning of circularity, requires that we all began in Christ and all shall end in Christ. Colossians 3 :11, reads, *"Where there is neither Greek nor Jew, circumcision nor uncircumcision, Barbarian, Scythian, bond nor free: Christ is all in all."*

In Genesis 1:1 it states that *"In the Beginning God (The Word),"* created the original heaven and the earth. All DNA, which is life, bears the signature of Christ. Every name has a signature. Every person has a name. Since Christ is all in all, we should be able to see His signature in the things that bear life and have DNA. In Colossians 1:15, Paul said, *"For by Him were all things created, that are in heaven, and that are in the earth, visible and invisible, whether they be thrones or dominions, or principalities, or powers: all things were created by Him."* I am going to show you some evidence of Christ's signature of life in creation, but before I do I will explain the Fibonacci sequence.

According to Wikipedia, *"Leonardo Pisano Bigollo known as Fibonacci –was an Italian mathematician considered by some to be the most talented Western mathematician of the Middle Ages. Fibonacci is best known for a number sequence named the Fibonacci numbers after him, which he did not discover but used as an example in the Liber Abaci (Book of Calculation)."* I want you to keep in mind that Fibonacci was not a Christian, he was a Catholic, and that he did not discover this. It was there all along, but he used it as an example. *Just like there are truths in the Bible that have been there all along but have been hidden.* The Fibonacci sequence is also called the *Golden Ratio* or even better *God's Ratio* (1:1.618). He found that by laying the numbers in cubes or blocks and drawing a spiral inside it, made a DNA pattern.

The Fibonaaci number sequence starts in the center and then continues to spiral out as the sum of each number is added to the last number and gets larger. Numbers are infinite and never end, and never change, just like GOD. It's funny because Haylael (Lucifer) knew how to stop the addition of the sum and seal it up so to speak. The first two numbers of the sequence are 0, and 1. Below is an example of the Fibonacci number sequence: *0 1 1 2 3 5 8 13 21 34 55 89 14 233 377 610 987 and etc.*

Haylael, Lucifer, or Satan was the anointed cherub that covereth (entwine, DNA strands), "He sealed up the sum, and was skilled in all wisdom concerning, calculating, counting, numbers, math science, chemistry, physics biology, zoology, and botany, as well as the ability to recognize patterns. He was a special being created with knowledge and afforded privileges that no one else had at that time." (More information about Haylael can be found in my first book, <u>Demons, Nephilim, and Angels. In Isaiah</u> 14: 12- 17 and Ezekiel 28: 12-19). Demons, Nephilim, and certain angels have DNA, God's signature.

Everything produced by God has life and has His signature. I'm not talking about the things that are man-made, like your house, car, clothes, material items, or things that were made by man's external manipulation. I'm speaking of the things that have been procreated and generate the power of life. The book of Psalm 19:1, informs us that, *"The heavens declare the glory of God; and the firmament sheweth His handywork."* Could this be why galaxies are circular shaped and seem to spiral out? This may very well be His handy work or His signature of life.

Consider the umbilical cord and it spiral shape. What about the top of the head, or our hair follicles? How they spiral out in a pattern. Even the very hairs on our head are numbered. This may be why the prophets wrote the words of the Lord on rolled up scrolls. How about roses and the way they spiral out? What about blades of grass and ocean waves? The Bible says, *"all flesh is as grass (Isaiah 40:6)."* These patterns must be His signature of life. The Bible even says GOD spoke out of the spiraling whirlwind in Job 38:1, *"Then answered the Lord out of the whirlwind, and said."*

Since Satan is a master musician it is no wonder that he knew that even musical notes have a spiral shape to them as well. How about our fingertips where DNA can be determined by fingerprints? They have that spiral pattern, GOD's DNA signature on them. Then there are sea shells, a chameleon's tail, and cauliflower. They have that spiral pattern, also. What about the human ear? It also has a spiral pattern. I need to elaborate in more detail to explain how man discovered DNA (Deoxyribonucleic Acid).

The true science of DNA was first discovered by Swiss physiological chemist, Friedrich Miescher, who called it, *"nuclein,"* which is inside the nuclei of human white blood cells. The term *"nuclein"* was later changed to *"nucleic acid"* and eventually to *"deoxyribonucleic acid,"* or *"DNA.,"* in 1953 by Francis Crick and James D. Watson. They discovered the double helix structure of DNA. This discovery would answer the mystery about living organisms.

According to Wikipedia, *"this mystery was the question of how it is possible that genetic instructions are held inside organisms and how they are passed from generation to generation."* Francis Crick helped to bring an understanding to genes, cells, and the genetic code in general, that all living organisms have DNA.

The DNA molecule is the instruction manual for the forming of amino acids and makes proteins for each individual parts of our bodies. There are 22 amino acids corresponding to the 22 Hebrew letters in the Aleph-Beth (where we get the word *Alphabet* from). The Hebrew word for protein connects to the word bar which means son, therefore, children or sons are the proteins made from the amino acids, *"The Word."*

The 22 letters represent the image of Jesus, who is *The Word* made flesh. In Isaiah 8:18, we are considered letters or words. *"Behold I and the children (Jesus and His body) whom the Lord has given me are for signs (letters) and for wonders in Israel, from the Lord of hosts, Which dwelleth in Mount Zion."* DNA is undoubtedly a picture of the Word. Since Christ is, *"The Word,"* made flesh.

He wants our (flesh) to become, *"The Word,"* here on the Earth, through His DNA.

According to Levi Madison, the letters of the DNA strand are comprised of Adenine, Guanine, Cytosine, and Thymine (A,T,C,G) . These four letters combined in pairs to make all the information needed to form life. Adenine always pairs with Thymine, and Guanine always pairs with Cytosine. In the Hebrew language all words come from two letter parent roots. Isaiah confirms this in Chapter 34 and verse 16, by stating, *"Search and read from the Book of the Lord (Yahweh); not one of these misses, each not lacking her mate; for He has commanded my mouth, and by His Spirit He has assembled them."*

As you can see the proper pairing and the proper mate are necessary, and it is done by The Holy Spirit. This description gives us a deeper picture of Christ and DNA. The 2-letter parent root can't be used in a sentence without the addition of a third letter (child root) called, codons. There is something in DNA that allows it to do this, and it is called RNA (Ribonucleic acid). RNA acts as a messenger and is an exact copy of the DNA molecule where the helix ladder "unzips" itself in order to make an exact copy. Levi Madison states, *"DNA is a picture of the Father on His throne (mercy seat (blood, DNA). The Messenger RNA is a picture of the Messiah who comes to earth to bring many sons to glory. This DNA to RNA and back to DNA process is seen on the work of the scribes, who made exact copies on the Torah (scroll, word). DNA works in the same way as the Hebrew language."*

In, *"DNA, Design, and the Origin of Life,"* Charles B. Thaxton informs us that, *"the genetic code can be best understood as an analogue to human language. It functions exactly like a code - indeed it is a code: it is a molecular communication system within the cell."* In an article on the Red Ice Creations website, in the article, entitled, *"Finding the Holy Grail,"* by Janae and Barry Weinhold. It declares, *"A team of Russian geneticists and linguistics, researching the electromagnetic behavior of DNA, discovered that "junk" DNA is critical not only for the construction of our body but also in data storage and communication. The Russian team discovered that this 90% of our DNA follows the same rules of grammar, syntax and semantics as human languages. Their conclusion is that human language mirrors the structure of our DNA."*

This just goes to show that the Word of God is more than letters, words, and sentences, it is literally the DNA of God. It is as if we have to unzip ourselves from the old sinful nature (DNA of Satan), and receive and copy the new man to this, sinless, blameless, spotless DNA.

Simply put the DNA strand is made of letters: ATGCTCGAATAATTGA. These letters make words: ATG CTC GAA TAA ATG TGA ATT TGA. These words make sentences: (ATG CTC GAA TAA) (ATG TGA ATT TGA). These sentences are called genes. Genes comes from the word Genesis. Genes tell the cells to make proteins. You can't add or take away from the DNA, otherwise a mutation results.

In Deuteronomy 12:32, Moses proclaims, *"All the things that I command you, take heed to do them, and you shall not add to it, nor take away from it."* Satan, demons, fallen angels, and or aliens work tirelessly trying to infiltrate, contaminate, and change our DNA by adding to our sentences in our bodies, or taking away from the word of God. Remember the parable in the books of Mark and Luke, Satan comes for the word. Look at Matthew 4:15, *"And these are they by the way side, where the word (logos) is sown; but when they have heard, Satan cometh immediately, and taketh away the word that was sown in their hearts."*

Mathematician, Murray Eden of MIT commented that, " DNA, like other languages, cannot be tinkered with by random various changes; if that is done, the result will always be confusion. No currently existing formal language can tolerate random changes in the symbol sequences which express its sentences. Meaning is invariably destroyed." We are told in Romans 12:2, to be *"transformed by the renewing of the mind."* The Greek word for *renewing* is; *anakainosis,* to regenerate or renovate by making something new or like new again, building back to a former, better state. This all occurs in the mind, which is Satan's primary battleground. The mind is changed or renewed when it receives new information. I know this may seem like a lot of information for the start of this book, but I need to lay the foundational understanding of DNA.

The English word information, originates from the Latin word *"informare,"* which means to train, instruct, form, and educate. When you break that word down, it means info, and forms a meaning of a physical form, shape or appearance. The Latin word, forma traces to the Greek word *morphe.* This is intriguing because the word transformed in the above verse means *metamorphoo* or *morph. Morphe* originates from the root word *"meros,"* which is defined as constituent parts to a hole., combining small parts to make an image. This is a description of the DNA becoming protein (image). Look at Mark 16:12, *"And after that he appeared in another form (morph) into the two*

16

of them, as they walked, and went into the country." This is a picture of Christ and His Resurrection DNA (blood). He changed forms. Let's call it a *"Manifestation of Favor."* This is a picture of the DNA set aside and portioned to us as joint heirs with Christ; making us into a special species, *"after His kind (species)."* *Morphe* is also connected to the Hebrew word *temunah,* which means living waters or blood, and links to the passing of genes from father to son through blood.

By hiding the secret of the knowledge of the adultery and mingling of DNA that took place in Eden's Garden is a major reason Satan keeps a stronghold on the church, (Bride of Christ).

By keeping the secret in the garden hidden, the rulers of darkness of this world can rule by false identity (DNA), which the church has been blinded to and allowed them to infiltrate the church and change its identity (DNA). The truth of the matter is that it is not about a snake and an apple. Nothing could be farther from the truth. It's about DNA. And you will realize that and more in the next chapter of, ***"Unveiling Secrets From Eden's Garden."***

2.
Shhh..........The Secret

Does God keep secrets that he hides, and we must seek? Well, according to scripture He does. The mystery of a secret is that one day it will be revealed. And many times, knowing something that we did not know before changes our Outlook on a matter. In Proverbs 25:2, one of my favorite passages states, *"It is the glory of God to conceal (hide) a thing: but the honour of kings is to search (to penetrate, find out, examine intimately) that matter out."* In order to find out God's concealed secrets, we must penetrate the matter and examine it intimately to discover and find out what is being veiled from sight. The Father wants to reveal His secrets to His prophets and His friends, but only to those who will search. *"The secret things belong unto the Lord our God: but those things which are revealed belong unto us and to our children forever."-Deut. 29:29.*

The Hebrew and Greek meanings of the word secret is to hide, be absent, conceal, hidden, protected, disguised, type, symbol, mystery, and parable. These are all code words for secret. The Holy Spirit has shown me a connection between the word secret and DNA. Let's analyze this word secret according to scripture before we proceed further.

DNA begins in the womb. If you read the first chapter you should remember that womb, covered, and umbilical cord are code words for DNA. Especially because the umbilical cord has that spiral shape that signifies God's signature. Look at *Psalm 139:13-15*. It reads, *13. "For thou hast possessed my reins: thou hast <u>covered</u> (entwine) me in my mother's womb." 14. I will praise thee; for I am fearfully and wonderfully made: marvelous are thy works; and that my soul knoweth right well. 15. "My substance was not <u>hid</u> from Thee, When I was made in <u>secret</u>..."* David acknowledged that our DNA is made in secret. I mean, think about it, in order to reproduce, the act of sexual intercourse with husband and wife are done in secret, in a room where it is just the two of them only. The secret place is where our DNA is stored, and it is not to be tinkered with, in any way. But we know from my first book that the devil pollutes, defiles, and manipulates DNA. Ezekiel puts it this way in chapter 7 verse 22, *"My face will I turn also from them, and they shall pollute My secret place: for the robbers shall enter in and defile it."*

It should not be defiled because it belongs to the Lord. All secrets belong to the Lord, waiting to be revealed to and through His true sons. So, what is this secret that has you all in suspense? Let's commence by looking at some clues from the Word of God that have been hidden in plain sight. What do you think Paul meant when he pointed us to Moses in II Corinthians chapter 3 verses 14-17? It reads, *14. "But their minds were <u>blinded (darkened)</u>; for until this day remaineth the same <u>vail</u> untaken away in the reading of the Old Testament; which vail is done away in Christ. 15. But even unto this day when Moses is read, the vail is upon their <u>heart</u> (thoughts, feelings). 16. Nevertheless* *when it shall __turn__ to the Spirit of the Lord, the vail shall be taken away. 17. "Now the Lord is that Spirit: and where the Spirit of the Lord is, there is liberty."* So, the key is in the Old Testament, specifically the books that Moses wrote.

The Spirit of the Lord has revealed the secret that is covered by a vail in Genesis. Once you understand Genesis, the rest of the books of the Pentateuch that Moses wrote will be understood when it is read and that will bring freedom. Apparently even the *Corinthians* and the *New Testament* Church had been ignorant of the *secret* in Genesis and specifically in the *Garden of Eden*. Think about *Moses* (to pull or draw out) and Saul (to ask for), and Paul (little humble), have specific and special meanings. For those who are humble and ask for the truth and will do the work of pulling and drawing it out of the word, will learn the secret.

Paul gave the Corinthians Clue # 2 as well. Survey II Corinthians 11:3, *"But I fear lest by any means, as the serpent BEGUILED Eve through his subtilty......."* I will be dissecting this verse later in this book, but for now it is utterly amazing how Paul uses the same words as Moses does in relating Eve's response to being questioned by The Lord God in Genesis 3, *"...the serpent BEGUILED me..."*

The word beguiled means to seduce wholly, lead astray. But I want you to focus on the word *seduction*. The truth of the matter is that word *seduce* can be defined as to entice into sexual activity. Wait a minute before you put this book down and dismiss this notion, please continue to read because the evidence is undeniable as I will lay it out like an attorney or more specifically defense attorney uncovering a lie by using evidence, witnesses and testimony. Remember most Christians are blind when reading Genesis according to Paul.

It will be shown that the secret is about DNA, not just genetic manipulation, but the transfer of DNA through sex. Clearly God wants to reveal secrets and He did so to Daniel (judge). God gives secrets to those that he can trust to judge them righteously by the word). Examine Daniel chapter 2:19, 22, *and 47. Verse 19. "Then was the secret revealed to Daniel in a night vision. Then Daniel blessed the God of Heaven." 22. "He <u>revealeth the deep (profound) and secret things:</u> He knoweth what is in the darkness and the light dwelleth with Him." 47. "The king answered unto Daniel, and said of a truth, it is that your God is a God of gods and a Lord of Kings, and a <u>Revealer of secrets</u> seeing thou couldest <u>reveal this secret.</u>"* It is evident that Daniel knew the secret. He even used one of the key words that I pointed out in the introduction, <u>seed</u>. The word seed has to do with DNA.

Let's explore Matthew chapter 13 which has the word seed 6 times in chapter 13 just as Genesis chapter 1 has the word seed 6 times. It is not a coincidence that Matthew (gift) has given us a gift in connecting the *secret* (DNA and sex) to the book of Genesis and the Garden of Eden.

The secret is revealed in Jesus' words, which he spoke to the multitudes in *parables*. (Remember *parable* is a key word for secret). He said in verse 35, *"I will open my mouth in parables; I will utter things which have been <u>kept secret (mystery) from the foundation (conception) of the world (the inhabitants began to flow).</u>"* The bible distinguishes the *"<u>world that then was</u>,"* (see, Demons Nephilim Angels book 1) from the world. The word *conception is defined as, a beginning, union of the sperm and ovum, fertilize,* and most importantly, *INCEPTION OF PREGNANCY.* These are things that have been kept hidden from (since) the inception of *pregnancy* (birth) of the inhabitants when they began to flow. Could Moses be referring to the pregnancy of Eve by Adam?

First of all, Adam did not know (have sexual intercourse) Eve until they were expelled from the garden. The Greek word for *seed* in this chapter is (get ready, wait for it....), *sperma*, where we get the English word *sperm*. The wheat are the good seed, or the children of God, and the tares are the bad seed or the children of the devil. Secondly let's look at this perplexing verse in Matthew 13:39, " the *enemy* that *sowed them* (seed, sperm, OFFSPRING) is the devil..." Wait a minute, offspring means children, and this is past tense. The devil extending his sperm and had children? YES!

Thirdly, for those who may say that Jesus was referring to *"spiritual"* children of Satan rather than literal, that's not a *secret*. It wouldn't be a mystery to the world, like He said He was revealing to His disciples. Would it? Why would He waste His time with something everyone already knew? Jesus was referring to Satan's literal descendants (Nephilim) with his DNA, and not just followers of Satan, and doers of evil.

Finally, Jesus pointed out to us the seed of the serpent, here. When Moses wrote in Genesis (Genes is... origin, life...) 3:15, *"And I will put enmity between thee (sperm, offspring) (the Serpent's seed) and the woman, and between thy seed and her seed; her seed (sperm, offspring) (The woman)."* I honestly don't comprehend why people get all bent out of shape because of the term *"serpent seed"* and label it a false doctrine? I am aware of the teachings of William Branham, but I am not a follower of him and I do not believe all his doctrine is correct on the matter. However, The Lord is talking to the serpent. Verse 14 says, *"And the Lord God said unto the serpent..."* So why would God speak of the serpent's sperm and offspring if he had none? Remember women don't carry the seed, the male does.

The woman's seed is the prophesied virgin birth of Jesus. But the Hebrew word for seed here is *zera,* meaning offspring or children. Look at this term *"seed"* in other instances in scripture to see if it is physical seed and children or spiritual seed. In *1 Samuel Chapter 20, verses 41and 42,* the phrase.. <u>*"between my seed and thy seed forever,"*</u> refers to a physical seed not spiritual. How about *1 Kings 2:33, "...and upon his* ^{seed} *forever....,"* this also relates to a physical seed. What about in referring to Jesus, who came as a physical seed? *Revelation 22:16 reads,"...the root and <u>offspring (seed)</u> of David?"* Serpent seed can't be spiritual in reference to scripture.

Can you see that the woman's seed and the serpent's seed are physical lines of descent that can be traced in scripture.? These two seeds will end in two Messiahs. One is counterfeit and the other is real, and spring from two different bloodlines. Now that we have laid an understanding about the secret and the correlation to the Garden of Eden and DNA, via sex, sperm, and offspring; we must unveil the truth about what occurred in the garden. But first we must see the evidence from the ***Revealer of Secrets,"*** on who this old serpent really was, and is.

3.

That Old Serpent Nacash

We need to go to the Word to find the origin and true identity of this *"Old"* serpent. The church and the world has been bamboozled into believing that this serpent was nothing more than a slithering, slimy snake who gave Eve an apple to eat and caused mankind to sin. However, it did not happen that way. If you take this traditional view of Genesis 3, how is it different from a child believing in Santa Claus, the Easter Bunny, or the Tooth Fairy? When Satan is called a serpent, how is it different from when Nero is called a *"lion,"* in II Timothy 4:17, or when Herod is called *"fox,"* in Luke 13:32. Did you know that snakes don't even have vocal chords? So how could a snake have spoken to Eve when it is not even possible?

The KJV Companion Bible appropriately states in Appendix 19, *"It is wonderful how a snake could ever be supposed to speak without the organs of speech, or that Satan should be supposed able to accomplish so great a "miracle." It only shows the power of tradition, which has, the infancy of each one of us, put before our eyes and written on our minds the picture of a "snake" and an "apple": the former based on a wrong interpretation, and the latter being a pure invention, about which there is not one word said in the Holy Scripture."* We have always

25

had this picture of a standing erect snake giving Eve an Apple when snakes do not even have the ability to speak.

So, let's go back to the beginning to find out about this serpent. In Revelation 12:9, it states, *"And the great dragon was cast out, that old serpent, Called the devil, and Satan, which deceiveth the whole world: he was cast out into the earth, and his angels were cast out with him."*

The word *"old"* means beginning or original. So, the Word is telling us that the serpent is the devil. In Ezekiel chapter 28 he is called the cherub that covers (entwine, like the DNA strands). In verse 3, it states there is no secret that is hid from thee. And remember secret is another call word for DNA. As we move down to verse 13 it states, *"thou hast been in Eden, the Garden of God..."* therefore it is clear that this serpent was in Eden, who is the devil. He is also called, *"Leviathan,"* and the meaning once again relates to DNA. In the Chapter 1, I referred to the *Fibonacci sequence (see the Chapter 1)* in God's signature of life. Look at this verse, *"In that day the Lord with His sore and great and strong sword shall punish Leviathan (a wreathed animal, serpent, to twine) the piercing SERPENT; and He shall slay the dragon that is in the sea. -Isaiah 27:1.*

The Hebrew word for *serpent* in Genesis 3:1 is *"ha Nachash."* The definition of this word is *to shine* or *"the shining one,"* and it also means brass or copper because of its shining nature. It comes from the word Seraph. Nacash, Seraph, and serpent have the same meaning. Cherubs can have the appearance of men at times, according to Ezekiel. So, the anointed angel who covers, can have the appearance of a beast at times as well. Isaiah chapter 6 describes the seraphim as coverer.

Therefore, you must keep in mind that he was not a

snake but a "*shining one.*" If you read my first book it was revealed that Lucifer means Haylael one who shines and boasts. The word serpent also means to whisper a magic spell, to enchant, and prognosticate (foretell the future). This goes to show the device he used to seduce Eve in the Garden. Based on this definition, we are given a clear understanding of this next statement from the companion Bible, *"We cannot conceive Eve as holding a conversation with a snake, but we can understand her being fascinated by an angel of light possessing superior and supernatural knowledge. It is wonderful how a snake could ever be supposed to speak without the organs of speech, or that Satan should be supposed able to accomplish so great a miracle. It only shows the power of tradition which has put before our eyes and written on our minds the picture of a snake and an apple; based on wrong interpretation and pure invention.* (Ap.19, The Companion Bible).

This book will be full of secrets that the Holy Spirit gave me to reveal. All of this began in the Garden of Eden. Instead of believing in fairytales, it is time for mature Christians to understand the unmitigated truth in Genesis about this serpent. Since we have established the meaning, I will refer to him as *"The Old Nachash."* I will also lay the foundation in Genesis 3:1, *"Now the serpent was more subtil (wise) than any beast (living creature) of the field which the LORD God had made. That word "subtle,"* also means cunning and bare and naked. Ezekiel chapter 28 verse 12 he told Satan he was full of wisdom.

Let's also look at that word beast. It means living thing or living creature. Therefore, *the old Nachash was wiser than any other living creatures which Jehovah Elohim* had made. It never states that Satan was a beast, but only states that he was wiser than any other living being.

This old Nachash, Satan, was demoted from his place in the mountain of God to be subservient to Adam in the Garden of God. Adam or mankind was to take his place in the mountain of God, have dominion over the Earth and subdue it. Of course, Satan is jealous of Man, because we are created in God's true image and have taken the place or position that he once held. The Old Nachash or serpent who beguiled Eve is spoken of as an angel of light in II Corinthians chapter 11 verses 3 and 14. This could not have been an upright talking snake with legs.

This is a supernatural being, a son of God, with the same ability to impregnate a woman that the sons of God (Watchers) who came down to earth in Genesis Chapter 6. The Old Nachash is the embodiment of all sin and corruption.

In numbers Chapter 21 the serpents mentioned were seraphs and were burning because of the poison of their bite and were called seraphs (burning). It is because of sin that the fiery flying serpents were sent to bite the children of Israel. But in verse eight of that same chapter the Lord commands Moses to make the fiery serpent and put it on a pole, symbolizing Jesus becoming sin and dying on a cross for us and our sins. Thank God for that tree or cross. Jesus, Basically, becoming as a serpent who represents sin to save us.

In the book of Acts chapter 5 verse 30, it states, *"The God of our fathers raised up Jesus, whom ye slew and hanged on a tree.* Then also in Galatians chapter 3 verse 13 we read, *"Christ hath redeemed us from the curse of the law, being made or becoming a curse for us: for it* *is written, cursed is everyone that Hangeth on a <u>tree</u>:"* and to further verify this matter we read I Peter chapter 2 verse 24, *"Who his own self bare our sins in his own body on the <u>tree </u>that we, being dead to sins, should live unto righteousness: by whose stripes ye word healed."* He had to literally die on the cross/tree.

Crosses look like the letter "X." The x is what the shape of a chromosome is like. He had to take on our human DNA to give us His DNA (the Blood of Jesus). So, the scriptures clearly tell us that He died on a tree, and that tree is associated with the serpent who is the devil, who is connected to sin. We must find out what the Holy Spirit is saying to us in the scriptures about trees. There must be more about trees than what we have been taught in the past.

4.

WALKING, TALKING, LIVING TREES

There is something peculiar about trees in the Bible. Have you ever wondered why in the first chapter of Genesis verse 29 God says to man, *"And God said, Behold , I have given you every herb bearing seed, which is upon all the face of the earth, and every tree, in the which is the fruit of a tree yielding seed; to you it shall be for meat? " –Genesis 1:29.*

And why God also tells man in Genesis chapter 2 verse nine, *"And out of the ground made the Lord God to grow every tree that is pleasant to the sight and good for food: the tree of life also in the midst of the garden, and the tree of the knowledge of good and evil?"- Genesis 2:9.* God tells the man he can eat from that he grew every tree that is good for food including the tree of the knowledge of good and evil. So why would God tell man in Genesis chapter 2 not to eat from the tree of knowledge of good and evil? There must be something going on with these *trees* and the word *"food."* The correlation must mean more than what we think, depending on the tree.

It's funny because when I was younger I used to watch a T.V. show called, *"HR Puff N Stuff."* On this show, in the forest, there were talking, walking, moving, living, breathing trees. I had always thought it was interesting and the image made an impression on me as a child. I believe the Holy Spirit imprinted that on my memory for this revelation that I am about to reveal. I do not think it is an accident when Mark chapter 8 verse 24, tells us Jesus laid his hands on the man to heal him of blindness, and the man said," I see men as trees walking." I believe that man saw into the spiritual world and was able to see the true nature of trees. Trees can be used in scripture as symbols and metaphors. There are many times in the word where trees are referred to as men.

When Nebuchadnezzar had a dream, Daniel interpreted the tree in the dream to be Nebuchadnezzar. In Daniel 4:20-22,*"The <u>tree</u> that thou sawest, which grew, and was strong... <u>it is that thou, O king</u>, that are grown and become strong..."* The tree in the dream was a metaphor for a man.

In Psalms Chapter 1 verse 3 it states, *"And he shall be like <u>a tree</u> planted by the rivers of water that brings forth fruit in <u>his</u> season; his leaf also shall not wither; and whatsoever <u>he</u> doeth shall prosper."* Pay attention to all the underlined words. They are proper pronouns that refers to a man or humankind.

If the above was not enough evidence for us, we can read in Ezekiel about these trees having an actual conversation. Ezekiel points out to us that these trees were in the Garden of God, not only the garden but the Garden of God which was in Eden; specifically. After reading the entire Chapter 31 in Ezekiel, reference is made to these trees by using the personal pronouns he, has, or himself. This is done so the reader can associate *trees with men.* It is an allegory of Satan lifting himself up, because of his beauty as a tree in the garden.

Our focus will be on Ezekiel chapter 31 verses 8, 9, and 18. observe 8. *"The cedars in the garden could not hide him: the fir trees were not like his boughs, and the chestnut trees were not like his branches; nor any tree in the Garden of God was like unto him in his beauty."* 9. *"I have made him fair by the multitude of his branches: so that all the trees of Eden that were in the Garden of God envied him."* 18. *"To whom art thou thus like in glory and in greatness among the trees of Eden? yet shalt thou be brought down with the trees of Eden unto the nether parts of the earth…"* *Ezekiel 31: 8,9,18.* These trees, particularly, the trees in the Garden of Eden were not all literal fruit trees.

In bring further evidence to this point about trees being like man, we will look at the book of Judges chapter 9. Even if it is an allegory, it is interesting that the author choses to use trees as an example of trees acting and talking like men. In Judges 9:8, *"The trees went forth on a time to anoint a king over them; and they said unto the olive tree, Reign thou over us."*

In Judges 9:10 – 15. In 10. *"And the trees said to the fig tree, Come thou, and reign over us. 11. But the fig tree said unto them, Should I forsake my sweetness, and my good fruit, and go to be promoted over the trees?" 12. Then said the trees unto the vine, Come thou, and reign over us. 13. And the vine said unto them, Should I leave my wine, which cheereth God and man, and go to be promoted over the trees? 14. Then said all the trees unto the bramble, Come thou, and reign over us. 15. And the bramble said unto the trees, If in truth ye anoint me king over you, then come and put your trust in my shadow: and if not, let fire come out of the bramble, and devour the Lebanon."* Even

God refers to Himself as a green fir tree in Hosea14:8. He says, *"I am like a green fir tree."*

The definition of the word tree is, *"Tree = ets, atash =, carpenter, stick, to fasten (or make firm), to close (the eyes): spine, through backbone (central nervous system giving you knowledge of good and evil). Jesus was a carpenter.* Look at the word spine. We know that refers to a backbone, or vertebrae. Men have backbones and spines. Can you see the correlation between the two?

It seems that there were many different types of trees that God created and made. There were indeed fruit trees according to Genesis 1:29. There were trees that were spiritual and represented beings. There were olive, fir, cedar, and oak trees as well. Then there were 2 special trees. The Tree of the Knowledge of good and evil and the Tree of Life. The Tree of the knowledge of good and evil represented Satan, and the flesh or physical realm. God did not want them to be aware of the flesh nor led by it.

Let's ponder what types of things that can be used for good or evil. Things such as the internet, money, robotics, and sex. Money can be used for good and evil, but sex is the most important of them all. Sex outside of marriage (between a man and a woman) is evil. But within a marriage it can be good. It is a feeling of lust versus the spirit of love. This love flows from the Tree of Life.

The Tree of of Life represented Jesus. Jesus is the way, the truth, and the life. So, the Tree of Life is Christ, and the way to eternal life is through Jesus and Him alone! The color green represents life, and that is a major reason that plants, trees, and grass are green. In Psalms 52:8, it says, *"But I am like a green olive tree in the house of God: I trust in the mercy of God for ever and ever."*

Is it a surprise that Jesus spoke to the fig tree as He cursed it? You probably are thinking, no it isn't. Jesus spoke to a lot of different things, including the wind and the waves. There is power in speaking the Word in faith. He even spoke to a fig tree in Mark 11: 12-14, *"And on the the morrow, when they were come from Bethany, He was hungry: And seeing a fig tree afar off having leaves, He came, if haply He might find anything thereon: and when He came to it, He found nothing but leaves; for the time of figs was not yet. And Jesus <u>answered</u> and said unto it No man eat fruit of thee hereafter forever. And his disciples heard it."*

Jesus' answer is a reply or a response, and in this case a reply to something said. Did the tree speak? Or is there a far more deep and fitting explanation; that trees represent people in scripture?

Now that the groundwork has been laid about trees, and in setting the scene. We shall see what really happened in the Garden of Eden or also called, the Garden of God? Was there some form of lusty ungodliness in the form of <u>intercourse</u> that occurred? Yes. Observe as the word unveils more truth.

5.

INTERCOURSE IN
THE GARDEN

Alright, to grasp this simple yet jaw dropping truth you are going to have to rid yourself of tradition. One of Satan's vices and methods is that God's children be deceived and believe a lie. The church has been and still blinded by **P**ride, **E**go, and **T**radition. There should be no *P.E.T.'s* allowed in the church because this blocks and quenches the move of The Holy Ghost.

There was a seduction and intercourse that took place in the garden. I am talking about sexual. First, let's look at what the Word depicts about what happened in the garden and we will then break down the etymology, definitions, and symbolism from this. Remember, keep in mind who this serpent is, as well as the tree of knowledge of good and evil. There are so many intricate secrets found in Genesis Chapter 3: 1-7 that are hidden in the original Hebrew and the meaning of the words that are used to give us details. For example:

1. " Now the serpent was more <u>subtil</u> (CUNNING) than any beast of the field which the LORD God had made. And he said unto the woman, Yea, hath God said, Ye shall not eat of every tree of the garden?

2. And the woman said unto the serpent, we may eat of

the fruit of the <u>trees of the garden:</u>

3. But of the fruit of the tree which is in the midst of the garden, God hath said, Ye shall not eat of it, neither shall ye touch it, <u>lest ye die</u>.

4. And the serpent said unto the woman, <u>Ye shall not surely die:</u>

5. For God doth know that in the day ye eat thereof, then your <u>eyes (33) shall be opened,</u> and ye shall be as gods, knowing good and evil. (46)

6. And when the woman saw that the <u>tree was good for food</u>, and that it was <u>pleasant to the eyes</u>, and a tree to be desired to make one <u>wise</u>, she took of the fruit thereof, and did <u>eat</u>, and <u>gave</u> also unto her husband with her; and he did <u>eat</u>.

7. And the <u>eyes</u> of them both were opened, and they <u>KNEW</u> they were <u>naked</u>."

Despite tradition, and popular opinion, this is not about them eating some apple or piece of fruit from a literal fruit tree and realizing that they were naked. Not to mention the walking snake that tempted them with words? No! This was a seduction. Can you picture a beautiful shining divine being, unlike any other in the garden that the eyes could behold? Picture him whispering sweet nothings into Eve's ear, enticing, suggestive, and seductive eye contact and body language. His immediate ambition was to put her into a spell, and an erotic trance, in the same way as a witch.

Before you put the book down, notice the following definitions: *The phrase <u>pleasant to the eyes</u> = <u>Hebrew word; chamad</u>: To* desire, to covet, to take pleasure in, to delight in, *The word <u>desired</u> = Hebrew word ta'avah (tah-av-aw');* from; to yearn for, *<u>to lust after</u>* (used of bodily appetites) a longing; or satisfaction. *To make one wise* = trees don't make you smart, but Satan can give you forbidden knowledge. *Wise*-insight. The word *took* = *Hebrew word laqach (law-kakh');* a primitive root; to take, lay hold of, to receive, *to marry*, to take a wife, *to procure,.*

Based on these meanings, Eve lusted after and yearned for this tree (Satan.) The word took means that she took him at that time for her husband and he took her as his wife. And you know what husbands and wives, do? Here is more proof:

The phrase *fruit of the tree* is Hebrew word *periy-*fruit, in a wide sense: a) fruit, produce (of the ground), or b) fruit, offspring, children, progeny (used of the womb), or figuratively c) fruit (of actions). The phrase *eat of it* is Hebrew word *'akal* (aw-kal'); This word has many uses, among which, one means to lay with a woman (which is a sexual act) *touch* is Hebrew word; *naga`* (naw-gah'); to touch, i.e. to lay the hand upon (for any purpose); euphemism for: to lie with a woman. Naked- nude, bare, cunning.

Fruit of a tree implies children and offspring. When she ate, it was a sexual act. Look at *Proverbs 30:20,* "Such is the way of an *adulterous woman*; she *eateth* and *wipeth* her mouth, and saith, I have done no wickedness." Adulterous is defined as voluntary sexual intercourse between a married person and a partner other than the lawful spouse (Adam). God married them in Genesis 2:24 and points out that the man and woman were naked and not ashamed because they had no *knowledge* of it. Why is an adulterous woman associated with eating and wiping the mouth? Another metaphor?

Consider another metaphor full of symbolism connected to the garden of Eden, from the Song of Solomon 2:3. *"As the apple tree among the trees of wood, so is my beloved among the sons. I sat down under his shadow with great delight, and his fruit was sweet to my taste."* It sounds like the serpent or tree of knowledge of good and evil.

And the Lord God said unto the woman, *"What is this that thou hast <u>done</u>? And the woman said, "The serpent <u>beguiled</u> me, and I did eat."* – In Genesis 3:13 <u>beguiled-nasha</u> – to lead astray, delude seduce wholly. <u>Seduce</u>-to tempt to wrong doing. Entice into illicit <u>sexual intercourse</u>. *"...for I have espoused you to <u>one husband,</u> that I may present you as a chaste <u>virgin</u> to <u>Christ</u>. But I fear, lest by any means, as the <u>serpent</u> <u>beguiled</u> Eve through his <u>subtilty</u>..."* II Corinthians 11:2.

Why does Paul refer to a <u>chaste</u> (abstaining from sexual intercourse) virgin? Eve was supposed to be presented to her husband as a virgin. In the same manner that the body of Christ should be presented to Christ in the same way. Quite simply put, a virgin is a person who has not experienced sexual intercourse. A virgin has no <u>knowledge of the good or evil</u> of sexual intercourse, especially since it's outside of marriage. Notice Paul also uses the word seduce. What do you think of when you hear or read the word seduce?

Another important thing to note is that each person is made up of DNA, which determines individual hereditary characteristics. God has a scroll with prescribed instructions that determine the development of my body, with all it's members in their proper order and sequence, from the embryo until the stage of maturity.

We are born with 46 chromosomes in total from both

of our parents. 23 from your mother, and 23 from your father. Even Jesus had 46 chromosomes even though He received 23 from Mary and 23 from The Holy Ghost. Jesus was conceived through the spoken word and not sex. Remember Mary was an unmarried virgin (her seed). The Word confirms the 46 chromosomes and the human body. Look at John 2:19-21. *19. "Jesus answered and said unto them, destroy this temple (DNA code word), and in three days I will raise it up. 20. Then said to the Jews, <u>46</u> years was this <u>temple</u> in building, and wilt thou rear it up in three days? 21. But the <u>temple</u> He spoke of was His <u>body.</u>"*

Satan, that Old Serpent or Nacash, spoke exactly 46 words to Eve. *"Yea, hath God said, Ye shall not eat of every tree of the garden? Ye shall not surely die: For God doth know that in the day ye eat thereof, then your eyes shall be opened, and ye shall be as gods, knowing good and evil (46),"* in Genesis Chapter 3:1-5. The Nacash was after DNA!

During his seduction and selfish act to attempt to infiltrate the DNA of the image of God in Eve, he wanted to infuse his seed into the bloodline of Christ while being lustfully enamored by Eve. And after witnessing the lamb being slain at the *"foundation of the world,"* he wanted to prevent or contaminate the bloodline.

After Haylel's unsuccessful attempt to genetically manipulate the DNA of God's creation in *"The World That Then Was,"* now the Nacash was in the garden. Eve (mother of all living) was a one-of- a -kind gorgeous creation, made from the DNA (deoxy*RIB* onucleic Acid) of Adam, and the likes of which no one had ever seen before, including that Old Nacash/Satan. He is a master musician, so I wouldn't be surprised if he didn't sing or play some romantic love songs, accompanied by slow jams and biorhythms that put her in a trance and cast his spell and get her in the mood, during his conniving foreplay.

Look at this statement, from Genesis 3, *"And when the woman saw that the <u>tree was good for food</u>, and that it was <u>pleasant to the eyes</u>, and a tree to desired to make one <u>wise</u>..., "* She was enticed by the <u>*lust*</u> *of the eyes, and the lust of the flesh* and wanted wisdom, because of *the pride of life* or a *divine nature,* which she already possessed. The word lust is mentioned twice. Lust is defined as intense or unrestrained sexual craving.

Eve abandoned her divine nature because of lust and was corrupted. Peter knew the secret when he spoke about lust in 1 Peter1:4. *"Whereby are given unto us exceeding great and precious promises: that by these ye might be partakers of the <u>divine nature,</u> having escaped the corruption that is in the world through lust. "* Eve thought that she could attain that glow by acting through her lust. She liked what she saw and was turned on by it, and so was that Old Nacash/Satan. *"...I was afraid, because I was naked and hid (secrete) myself."* –Genesis 3:10.

I noticed that Adam responded first and said that he hid himself because he was naked. What do married couples (man and woman) do together when they are naked? The word hid means to secrete. Secrete has two meanings. The first definition is to conceal in a hiding place, but the second has a more significant meaning, to release bodily fluids, such as *sperm.* The word <u>*secrete*</u> is all about secrets. It means both *"to hide,"* and *"to release."* Just as the penis is hidden and designed for one thing and one thing alone, to *"release"* You can see the word secret in the word secrete. When you squeeze a lemon, it secretes juice that is secretly hidden inside of the lemon.

Before I explain the circumstances for Adam's secretion, we should go back and look at some facts hidden in plain sight. God cursed the woman in the area where she gives birth, the genital area. If her sin was not about her eyes (senses being opened to the flesh) through an affair with that Old Nacash/Satan, then why would God do this? Let's look at Genesis 3.

"...I will greatly multiply thy <u>sorrow</u> (labor, pain) and thy <u>conception (pregnancy)</u> (9,46)..in sorrow shall you bring forth children and thy <u>desire</u> shall be to thy husband..."-Genesis 3:16. The ninth word in that verse is conception, and it is no wonder that it takes 9 months for a child to be born after conception. He is addressing a pregnancy that has occurred as a result of intercourse with that *tree* or Nacash. Here is what really happened in the Garden of Eden: Eve lost her virginity to 'the *serpent,'* who was that *<u>"Tree of the knowledge of good and evil in the midst of the garden."</u>* Who is none other than Satan himself. Also, God says her *desire* (stretching out, to run after) will be to her husband, because it was then when she desired that Old Nacash/Satan and stretched out to him in order to eat (lay) with him bearing his (fruit) offspring.

Adam and Eve covered their genitals and backsides, not their mouths. If it was about eating an apple, then why didn't they tape their mouths closed? This act displays how they were ashamed of what they did with those *secret* body parts and covered them. That's why they are referred to as *"private parts."* Because they are kept in secret. If it was about what they literally ate why didn't they cover their mouths? It reads, *"...and they knew that they were naked... and made aprons."* Gen. 3:7.

Another secret in scripture lies in the fact that they used fig leaves. It is funny because in God's pharmacy the fruit or vegetable that aids a certain body part resembles that body part. When you cut a carrot open it looks like a human eye, and it is not a secret that carrots help the eyes and sharpen vision. To be frank, figs look like testicles. On top of that very obvious fact, figs are full of seeds and *hang in twos* when they grow.

Figs increase the mobility of male sperm and increase the numbers of Sperm as well to overcome male sterility. They covered themselves with their shame, guilt, and sin, and that would never do. What they needed to be covered with is in Ephesians 6:14, *"Stand therefore having your loins (reproduce, beget and conceive offspring) girt (to join by a yoke) about with truth......"*

Our Heavenly Father prophetically slain a lamb from the conception or foundation of the world, for the inhabitants, for Adam (mankind). In Genesis 3:21, we read, *"Unto Adam also and to his wife did the LORD God make coats of skins and clothed them."* It was coats of the skins of the lamb that was slain to cover their sinful act. Could it be a coincidence that most condoms are made from lambskin? Lambskin condoms are made to prevent pregnancy, and prevent offspring, as well as *protection* from sexually transmitted diseases. Did the Nacacsh give Eve an STD? Of course, it had to start in the garden. Adam, Eve and their children needed protection from that Old Nacash or Serpent.

Please don't forget that God put hate and strife between that Old Nacash's/Satan's seed (sperm, offspring, child), and the woman's. He is speaking of a literal child. This is more evidence of a sexual affair that took place in the

Garden. Now let's get back to Adam's secretion in the Garden.

I am sure that if you are not in shock from this glaring, misquoted and misunderstood truth, that your next question is, well if Eve had sexual intercourse with this tree and that Old Nacash/Satan, then what about Adam, after he ate (lay) also? Well, the answer relates to his secretion and why he hid himself, because of the shame of what he did. Let's begin here.

How could Adam let Eve commit this sin? The Bible says, in Genesis 3:12, *"And the man said, the woman whom thou gavest to be with me, she gave me of the tree and I did eat (lay)."* Was Adam with her when this happened and chose not to intervene? Or was she by herself, seduced and taken advantage of?

If you recall, to extract DNA (Deoxy *RIB*- onucleic Acid), not a literal rib from Adam to make woman, God performed the first surgery and put Adam in a deep sleep, to remove some of his DNA. *"And the LORD caused a deep (lethargy, trance) sleep to come upon Adam and he slept..." (Genesis 2:21).* After he woke up, he proclaimed, "This is now bone of my bones, and flesh of flesh: she shall be called Woman because she was taken out of Man." Eve was made from his flesh and bone (DNA). He told her everything that God said, went back into a deep sleep to recover from surgery.

I have had surgery, because of the anesthesia, and toll that it took on my body, I know that right after, even days and weeks after surgery, I was sore and lethargic. Lethargy means to be sluggishness, inactivity, and a state of unconsciousness resembling deep sleep. So, yes, he was there with her, but he was in a deep sleep. And to top it off the scripture states, *"...and gave also to her husband WITH HER; and he did eat."*

Jesus gives us another hint in Matthew 13:25, *"But while men slept, his enemy came and sowed (sperma, male sperm) tares among the wheat..."* God's children are the wheat. Satan's children are the tares.

This leaves one to ponder, when Eve woke him, did he willingly participate in intercourse with that Old Nacash/Satan, who disguised himself as a transgender woman. One would believe that since the power of lust drove Eve, Adam must have fell victim as well. Haylael had this androgynous beauty to him/her. That's why he is associated with Transgender Baphomet that is both female and male. It is also both human and beast.

There is a term or terms that express Lucifer also as *Lucifera. Lucifera* refers to the planet Venus and is the female side of the devil. We know that Adam wasn't deceived, so he voluntarily engaged in sex to satisfy his curiosity. He became aroused, excited and ejaculated on the ground. Lust is a strong feeling, because the flesh is in complete control. As raw and unbelievable as this may seem, I believe Adam had enough sense not to let Satan obtain his sperm (DNA) to duplicate God's precious creation, himself, or humankind. Because of this atrocious act of disobedience, God cursed the ground for Adam's *sake.* The very ground that he secreted on.

When you look at some of the definitions for the word *sake* it seems to make even more sense. The ground was cursed for Adam's *sake (transition, crossover, gender, to cover in copulation)* in Genesis 3:17. This makes me question if a homosexual act occurred between he and Satan causing Adam to spill his seed on the ground???

Homosexuality had to begin in the garden and this seems to be when it occurred.

As we see the rise in transgenderism in America today, it fits. Upon writing this book, transgender man, Bruce Jenner, turned into Caitlyn Jenner, was voted woman of the year. The problem with that is, he was born a woman. Under Barak Obama's presidency transgenders were given preference and even allowed to use the restroom, and locker room facilities of their choice. In the coming days many posing as a woman or a man will be exposed to be the exact opposite gender of what we thought. Many in the private sect, but many more celebrated people who are icons in the public view.

God created them male and female and made man and woman. Why? Because it is about gender. He creates a male spirit to put into a man's body and a female spirit to be put into a woman's body. God does not make mistakes and does not operate in confusion. Animals are not classified as man and woman, but male and female. When God brought the animals into the ark, they came in by sevens for sacrifice and by two's (male and female) to replenish the earth. One of the definitions for sake is to cover the ground in copulation.

Copulation is a joining together through sexual intercourse and to transfer male reproductive cells (sperm) from one individual to another. In this case it was transferred to the ground, from Adam. Is it possible that Satan transformed himself into the appearance of a woman pretending to have a womb? Homosexuality and transgenderism secretly started in the Garden of Eden among other things. Now you are seeing the unveiled truth about what really happened in the Garden.

As shocking as it might seem, intercourse took place in the Garden. The secret of the knowledge of the adultery and mingling of the DNA that took place in Eden's Garden is a major reason Satan keeps a stronghold on the church, (Bride of Christ). By keeping the secret in the Garden hidden, the rulers of darkness of this world can rule by false identity (DNA), which the church has been blinded to, and allowed them to infiltrate the church to change its identity (DNA). It's almost like producing a fake birth certificate for a fake identity. Eve had sex with the Old Serpent or shining one. She was impregnated by him. We are not told if Eve and Adam had any sexual intercourse before she was impregnated by the Old Serpent. Satan was successful in infiltrating God's DNA, as he and Eve engaged in fore-play, and then intercourse that led to a baby.

By the time, we are told that Adam knew (had sex) with his wife, Eve, she was already pregnant with that Old Nacash/Satan's baby, Cain. I bet you are wondering, how that is possible since Cain and Abel were twins, and it is widely believed that Adam is Cain's father?

6.

Heteropaternal Superfecundation

For everyone who believes that it is impossible for Eve to have twins by two different fathers (one of them being The Nacash/Satan/Serpent), there is a technical term for this. It's called H*eteropaternal Superfecundation.* The definition of this term is the same cycle by sperm from two different males of fraternal twins. There are 7 -10 documented cases in medical history about fraternal twins with different fathers. Fraternal twins are one of a pair of twins, not necessarily resembling each other, or of the same sex, that develop from two separately fertilized ova.

One of the most recent cases of heteropaternal superfecundation involved women on the Maury Povich's Show in 2007 and 2008. A woman named, Regina contacted the Maury Show to try to prove that her ex-boyfriend, Jose, was the father of her twins. Maury said, *"The show has been very dramatic and a very edgy theme which I think are played out in American society. The most unusual dramatic DNA theme was when the woman came on the show and found out that her twins had different fathers."* Then Povich read out the DNA results and announced that Eric was the father of just one of her twins, he had to explain to a visibly shocked audience that this was not beyond the realms of possibility.

When it happened a second time on the show in 2008, to both 19 years old, Alejandrina and her ex-boyfriend, Jose, Maury was armed with the facts. He said: *'I want to explain about this situation. It has happened before on this show with fraternal twins. Less than one per cent of fraternal twins are from different fathers, to be accurate 0.001 per cent of the time and this is one of those less than one per cent.'* This occurrence is so uncommon that only a few cases have been documented in medical records. In rare instances when twins are conceived by different fathers, it's called *heteropaternal superfecundation,* which occurs when two or more of a woman's eggs are fertilized by different men within the same ovulation period. Before the results were read out, Alejandrina promised that she had not slept with anyone else while she was with Jose, and broke down in tears when the truth came out.

Read more: http://www.dailymail.co.uk/news/article-1378184/Woman-discovers-twins-sons-DIFFERENT-fathers-The-Maury-Show.html#ixzz3spDyoSs7

Read more: http://www.dailymail.co.uk/news/article-1378184/Woman-discovers-twins-sons-DIFFERENT-fathers-The-Maury-Show.html#ixzz3spDNgYPw .

If that is not compelling enough, it also happened again recently, in May 2009. A Texas woman wasn't planning on two conceptions for the record books. But that's what she got- along with two beautiful boys — when she gave birth to twins with different fathers nearly a year ago.*"Both of them have similar appetites. They like to play with their older brothers. They like to play with each other,"* Mia Washington told the TODAY show. How did that happen?

"Every month a woman's ovary releases one egg that can be fertilized by one sperm. But in this case, a pair of eggs emerged. Sperm, meanwhile, can remain alive and well and viable for up to five days in the reproductive tract. Thus, a woman can have sex with different men within those five days and the sperm just kind of hangs out there waiting for the egg to be released," according to Dr. Hilda Hutcherson, Clinical Professor of Obstetrics and Gynecology at Columbia University. She told this to Meredith Vieira on the TODAY Show.

Washington, who just turned 20, admitted to her partner that she had sex with another man within that five-day window — hence, the double conception. The mystery began to be solved when her partner, 44-year-old James Harrison, became concerned that Justin and Jordan, born only 7 minutes apart, looked so different. A paternity test followed. http://www.today.com/parents/working-moms-prioritizing-time-crucial-2D80555028.

You can clearly see, that it is even possible and occurs even today. If you read Genesis 3 and 4 closely, after God pronounced judgment; Then, Adam *KNEW*(sexually) his wife. A husband should know his wife and vice- versa because knowing implies love, intimacy and making love, as opposed to eating or laying in lust, and having sex outside of marriage between a *MAN* and a *WOMAN*. Before I proceed with more evidence of paternity in the

Garden, I want to clear up what the true meaning of the pronounced judgment on that Old Nacash/Satan was.

Look at Genesis 3:14, *"And the LORD God said unto the serpent (nacash, shining one), Because thou hast done this, thou art cursed above all cattle, and above every beast of the field; upon thy belly shalt thou go, and dust shalt thou eat all the days of thy life:* I know that many in the church believe that this walking snake was cursed to slither around on his belly, as the modern and traditional snakes that are seen today. But I don't believe that is what this means. I mean really, we have already undoubtedly identified from the Bible that Satan is the Serpent. So, what good would it do to curse Satan as a slithering snake, and continue to allow him the ability to transform himself into different things? There is also the fact that Satan in scripture is said to be, <u>*walking up and down in the Earth,"*</u> and <u>*"walking to and fro in the Earth."*</u> He is walking, and not crawling on his belly. Appropriately, the Lord cursed him to go on his belly, to represent the curse that he (the Serpent) put in Eve's belly.

The word belly here means, *belly, as the source of the fetus, labor to bring forth.* Since he wanted to lay with Adam as a woman, from that point forward his gender would be a putrid circle of confusion, as is the case with the transgender people. A transgender man can't have children. Although, as of today, they are working on some sort of technology to manipulate this truth and human DNA. *"In The Beginning God"* created everyone to be the exact gender they were when they were born. Their gender matches their spirit and personality.

The phrase or expression, *"upon thy belly shalt thou go,"* is a Hebraic figure of speech or an idiom for utter defeat as in Ps 72:9 and in Isa 49:23. It is the utmost humiliation. Meaning an ultimate term of degradation, as in Ps. 44:25 castration? Yes, this is what I believe happened. That Old Nacash/Satan was castrated. Castration can be labeled as the ultimate humiliation for a man. Castration is to remove the testicles of a male, to remove the ovaries of a female or to deprive of virility or spirit. He also had his counterfeit female reproductive organs removed. He posed as a transgender woman to try to hijack Adam's seed, but Adam had enough sense to spill it on the ground, inadvertently causing the ground to be cursed.

This androgynous hermaphrodite was rendered sterile *(I always wondered why he was called beautiful, instead of handsome. Woman are called beautiful. Men are called handsome).* This was done to crush his ego and to ensure that whatever he transformed himself into, whatever creature, male or female, he would not be able to reproduce in any manner whatsoever.

"He that is wounded in the stones, or hath his privy member cut off, shall not enter into the congregation of the Lord." – Deut. 23:1. Privy member is *shophkah, a pipe for pouring forth, penis, to spill forth, gush out.* These are all Hebraic definitions from the Word of God. Ezekiel says Satan was cast as *profane* out of the mountain of God. The word profane is defined in this verse as opening a wedge, prostitute, and perforated pipe. Remember in *Isaiah 14:13,* after his expulsion from Heaven, and his seat on the Divine Council, he said...."*I will sit also upon the mount of congregation..."* Well he couldn't for a number of reasons, and one of them is found in Deuteronomy 23.

Now that we have clarity on *his belly,* let's return to the paternity of those twins. I want to be clear, I don't believe in the races as being Black, Latino, Native American, Caucasian, and Asian, etc. There are different *ethnicities* as the word puts it. It is the word "*nations*," which is the Greek word "*ethnos,*" and it means, a people, the human race. Therefore, we are all of one race and one blood according to Acts 17:26, *"And hath made of one blood all nations of men..."*

There is another race or offspring and that is the race of the serpent. *".... for out of the serpent's root shall come a cockatrice (poisonous serpent), and his fruit shall be a fiery flying serpent."- Isaiah 14:29.* The serpent has a root (offspring, race) and fruit (offspring). The seed of the serpent. There is the human race and the Serpent's/Satan's race, and they look the same. And are in the same skin. But with different DNA. This is exemplified in Matthew and the parable (secret) of the wheat and the tares; they look exactly alike. This was the case with Cain and Able. Or was it?

I learned years ago that *punctuation is powerful.* Especially in the word of God. We can often read the bible the wrong way at times, missing deeper revelation, and neglecting the presence, usage, and or lack of punctuation. I will give you a worldly example and a biblical one. First the worldly, "An English professor wrote the words..."*a woman without her man is nothing"* .... On the whiteboard and asked his students to punctuate it correctly. All of the males in the class wrote: *"a woman, without her man, is nothing."* All the females in the class wrote: *"a woman: without her, man is nothing."* That's a quote from David Avocado Wolfe.

So, from there you can see the power in punctuation and its interpretation. In the Bible, which simply starts with Genesis chapter 1 verse one. In this verse the lack of punctuation makes a difference in my opinion. I believe it should of been a comma placed in the first sentence of the Bible. When you read, *"In the beginning God created the heavens and the earth."* As you read it this way as it is displayed in the Bible it seems as if it is talking about just time as the beginning. But when you add a comma and read it this way. *"In the beginning God, created the heavens and the earth."* This shows *the beginning God* as *a person* who we all know is the *word* as John chapter 1 confirms.

All right, I laid all of that groundwork to show you this next passage of Scripture. *"And Adam knew his wife; and she conceived and bare Cain and said I have gotten a man from the "LORD."* Why use a semicolon here, as opposed to just a comma? Adam knew his wife and right, after that she gave birth. The semicolon is a punctuation mark that separates some major sentence elements. A semicolon can be used between two closely related independent clauses. That is why it has a period and a comma. A comma is used because there is a but separating the two clauses. *Adam knew his wife, but she conceived and bare Cain.* A period is used because the two clauses can stand alone. *Adam knew his wife. She conceived and bare Cain.*

The Lord confirms his word with truth. If you wanted to say Adam knew his wife, she conceived and bare Cain. There is no use or need of the semicolon. I believe that (;) there, speaks volumes to what was happening. In the next verse it says, *"And she again bare his brother Abel..."* That word again means repeatedly as a connected act, and to continue to do a thing. They were not identical twins but fraternal twins. In *Genesis 4:25*, Moses shows us, *"And*

Adam <u>knew</u> his wife <u>again</u> ..." Here you see the word *<u>again</u>* to show the act already happened. In Genesis 4:2, it just says, *"Adam knew his wife..."* and this reveals that this was the first time that Adam knew his wife; not in the Garden. All of this is supported by the evidence of Scripture and the unmitigated fact that Cain is not mentioned in the genealogy and bloodline of Adam.

7.

BLOODLINES:
HIS DNA vs HER DNA
(SEED vs SEED)

Have you heard that old cliché? *"Blood is thicker than water."* Well it is. There are a few things that imply a stronger connection than blood. DNA or *life is in the blood* according to Leviticus 17:14. Another word for bloodlines is genealogy, and it is a record or table of the descent of a person, family, or group from an ancestor or ancestors, or a family tree.

Cain is not mentioned in the lineage of Adam because he was not Adam's seed, but of another, as we read in I John 3:12: *"Not as Cain, who was of that wicked one, and slew his (half) brother..."* Here the word "*of*" in Greek is in the Strong's Concordance. When used implying a person, it means *"a son of or off spring. "*

Genesis Chapter 5 begins as follows, *"This is the book of the <u>generations</u> (genealogy, bloodline, family tree) of Adam...."* As a matter of fact we are given the distinct and separate record of the genealogy of Cain in Genesis Chapter 4:17-24 *"And Cain knew his wife; and she conceived, and bare Enoch: and he builded a city, and called the name of the city, after the name of his son, Enoch. 18. And unto Enoch was born Irad: and Irad begat Mehujael: and Mehujael begat Methusael: and Methusael* *begat Lamech. 19. And Lamech took unto him two wives: the name of the one was Adah, and the name of the other Zillah. 20. And Adah bare Jabal: he was the father of such as dwell in tents, and of such have cattle. 21. And his brother's name was Jubal: he was the father of all such as handle the harp and organ. 22. And Zillah, she also bare Tubal-cain, an instructer of every artificer in brass and iron: and the sister of Tubal-cain was Naamah. 23. And Lamech said unto his wives, Adah and Zillah, Hear my voice; ye wives of Lamech, hearken unto my speech: for I have slain a man to my wounding, and a young man to my hurt. 24. If Cain shall be avenged seventy-fold, truly Lamech seventy and sevenfold."* Cain's name is nowhere to be found in the entire chapter of the book of the record of the genealogy of Adam.

Adam's genealogy can be found in Genesis 5:1-32," *This is the book of the generations of Adam. In the day that God created man, in the likeness of God made he him; 2. Male and female created he them; and blessed them, and called their name Adam, in the day when they were created. 3. And Adam lived an hundred and thirty years, and begat a son in his likeness, after his image; and called his name Seth: 4. And the days of Adam after he had begotten Seth were eight hundred years: and he begat sons and daughters: 5. And all the days that Adam lived were nine hundred and thirty years: and he died. 6. And Seth lived and hundred and five years, and begat Enos: 7. And Seth lived after he begat Enos eight hundred and seven years, and begat sons and daughters: 8. And all the days of Seth were nine hundred and twelve years: and he died. 9. And Enos lived ninety years, and begat Cainan: 10. And Enos lived after he begat Cainan eight hundred and fifteen years, and begat sons and daughters: 11. And all the days of Enos were nine hundred and five years: and he died. 12. And Cainan lived seventy years, and begat Mahalaleel: 13. And Cainan lived after he begat Mahalaleel eight hundred and forty years, and begat sons and daughters: 14. And all the days of Cainan were nine hundred and ten years: and he died. 15. And Mahalaleel lived sixty and five years, and begat Jared: 16. And Mahalaleel lived after he begat Jared eight hundred and thirty years, and begat sons and daughters: 17. And all the days of Mahalaleel were eight hundred ninety and five years: and he died. 18. And Jared lived and hundred sixty and two years, and he begat Enoch: 19. And Jared lived after he begat Enoch eight hundred years, and begat sons and daughters: 20. And all the days of Jared were nine hundred sixty and two years: and he died. 21. And Enoch lived sixty and five years, and he begat Methuselah: 22. And Enoch walked with God after he begat Methuselah three hundred years, and begat sons and daughters: 23. And all the days of Enoch were three hundred sixty and five years: 24. And Enoch walked with God: and he was not; for God took him. 25. And ethuselah lived an hundred eighty and seven years, and begat Lamech: 26. And Methuselah lived after he begat Lamech seven hundred eighty and two years, and begat sons and daughters: 27. And all the days of Methuselah were nine hundred sixty and nine years: and he died. 28. And Lamech lived an hundred eighty and two years, and begat a son: 29. And he called his name Noah, saying, this same shall comfort us concerning our work and toil of our hands, because of the ground which the Lord hath cursed. 30. And Lamech lived after he begat Noah five hundred ninety and five years, and begat sons and daughters: 31. And all the days of Lamech were seven hundred seventy and seven years: and he died. 32. And Noah was five hundred years old: and Noah begat Shem, Ham, and Japheth."*

I'm sure you felt, like I used to, that reading the begats can be boring, but God put them there for a reason. Did you also notice that some of the names on Cain's genealogy chart are very similar to the names on Adam's family tree? Those names are significant, have a message and a meaning as you will see later. God wanted us to see the separation, the war and the hatred between Adam and Eve's descendants and the Serpent's descendants.

And I will put <u>enmity</u> (hate) between thee and the woman, and between <u>thy seed (child)</u> and <u>her seed</u> (?) it shall bruise thy head and thou shalt bruise his heel. - Genesis 3:15.

It can be seen here how the Lord is making a separation between the two bloodlines and prophesying a curse of hate between the two. It
is first witnessed in Genesis chapter 4 that Cain hates Abel, because his offering was not accepted of the Lord and his Abel's was. I also believe that Cain was jealous of Abel, because Adam was his biological father and not Cain's. Abel may have even looked different than Cain resembling Adam.

The Lord is talking about both a physical seed and spiritual seed which I addressed earlier. Just like we are adopted into the bloodline of Jesus spiritually. There is also a physical bloodline of Jesus. Anyone can be adopted into the bloodline of Satan, but there is a literal bloodline of that Old Nacash/Satan. Adoption means to take into one's family through legal means, to raise as one's own child, or to vote to accept.

Cain had so much enmity against his brother that he killed him in Genesis 4:8, *".... Cain rose up against his brother and <u>slew him</u>. (enmity) 9. And the Lord said unto*

Cain <u>where is Abel thy brother?.. I know not. Am I my brother's Keeper?</u> "10"What has thou done? <u>the voice</u> of thy brother's blood cries from the ground. 11. And now art <u>thou cursed from the (face of) earth</u> which hath <u>opened her mouth</u> to receive thy brother's blood from thy hand. 16. And Cain went out from the <u>presence (face)</u> of the Lord, and dwelt in the land <u>of Nod (wander, disappear)</u> 17. And Cain knew his wife...."- Genesis 4:8-17. But where did Cain find his wife?

I believe there were other trees on the earth or people before Adam and Eve. Where could he have found his wife if no one else existed. Remember trees are metaphors in scripture.

I believe from the inquisition of the Lord that Cain engaged in *cannibalism* and ate his brother and tried to bury his bones. I believe that's why his blood cried from the ground. Where was his body? If you combine the two words Cain and Abel, like this; *cainabel*, it sounds like the word *cannibal*. This may be where the word and practice come from. Could this also be a trait in the DNA of his daddy, when it was prophesied to that old acash/Satan, *"dust shalt thou eat?"*

Vampires feed on the blood of living things by sucking the life out of their victims. Unbeknownst to many people in the movie series, *"Twilight,"* no matter how fascinating the story, is about vampires. Look at these verses. 23. *Only be sure that thou <u>eat not the blood</u>: for the <u>blood is the life;</u> and thou mayest not eat the life with flesh. 24. Thou shalt not eat it; thou shalt <u>pour it upon the earth as water.</u> 25. Thou shalt not <u>eat it;</u> that it may go <u>well </u>with thee, and with thy <u>children after thee,</u> when thou shalt do that which is right in the sight of the Lord. Deuteronomy 12:23-25.* Eating human flesh and drinking blood is not of God.

It is a satanic occult ritual that The Nacash requires his children and followers to perform for control and power. This sounds similar to what the Nacash's son Cain did by killing Abel.

It is also an insult to our Lord and Savior Jesus Christ because we take Holy Communion and partake in the Lord's supper and eat the body and consume the blood of the Lord. Satan has always been a copycat and always will be. Even if you look at the table below you'll see some of the names in Cain's pedigree are identical to the names in Adam's pedigree.

Remember after Cain killed Abel, Seth was appointed as a replacement for the seed of the bloodline for Jesus to come through to remain pure. It's confirmed by Eve's own words, *"And Adam* knew *his wife* again; *(repeatedly); and she bare a son, and called his name Seth (appointed, granted) For God, said she, hath appointed me (Seth) another seed (son) instead of Abel, whom Cain slew,"* Genesis 4:25. In the chart below, there isa hidden message in the pedigrees in the meaning of their names, and shows that there is power and meaning in names.

For Cain the prophetic message is, *"the possession brought forth shall be initiated or dedicated in teaching Babylon or confusion. He will be a fugitive smitten of God and a man of God, who is powerful, but beautiful and shady, skilled in music and brass and iron and false loveliness.*

For Adam the prophetic message is, *"a man reported to become a substitute born as a mortal man in a nest of sorrow. He will be the praise and glory of God come down from heaven, initiated and dedicated in teaching His death shall be powerful and bring rest and comfort."* (The death of Jesus)

Genealogies are compiled to show biological descent, the right of inheritance, succession to an office, or ethnological and geographical relationships. When we choose Jesus, we receive His bloodline and blessings.

Basically, His DNA. Living like Cain and his bloodline, you receive curses. On the next page you will see the names of Cain's family and Adam's bloodline and what message their names give us.

Cain's Geneolgy

Cain- possession (brought forth)
Enoch-initiated, dedicated, (teaching)
Babylon
Irad- fugitive, fleet
Mehujael- smitten of God
Methusael- a man who is of God

Lamech- powerful 666yrs.
Adah – beauty

Zilla-shade

Jabel - stream (tents, cattle)

Jubal- music, Harp, organ
Tubal-Cain- Alchemy, Artificer in
Brass and iron – FLOWS FORTH
Naamah - loveliness
"The Mason must follow in the
footsteps of his forefather
Tubal-Cain, Vulcan of
the Pagans."-Manly P. Hall

Adam's Geneology

Adam- mankind, red, (man)
Seth- substituted, –
appointed)
Enos-mortal man
Cainan- a nest , (sorrow)
Mahalaleel –praiseof God
(The Glory of God)
Jared –descend, come down
Enoch- initiated, dedicated,
(teaching)
Methuselah- man of dart,
sword,missile (His death
shall bring)
Lamech- powerful 777 yrs.
Noah- rest, comfort (perfect
in his generations (DNA)

Leviticus states, *"that life is in the blood."* Generational curses and blessings run through bloodlines. There is evidence of Cain's bloodline having iniquity. Iniquity is defined as perversity, evil, or sin. Look at Exodus 34:7, *"Keeping mercy for thousands, forgiving <u>iniquity</u> and transgression and sin, and that will by no means clear the guilty; visiting the iniquity of the fathers upon the <u>children</u>, and upon the <u>children's children</u>, unto the <u>third and fourth generation</u>."*

Thanks to the precious and dynamic blood of Jesus we can be washed free from sin and have generational curses that affect us through our DNA eradicated. After that the generational blessings can be activated in our lives to affect our DNA. There are secret curses and blessings in every family's bloodline that need to be addressed, confronted, renounced, bound or loosed. Throughout the Old Testament, Our Heavenly Father went to and allowed great and unique lengths to preserve and protect the bloodline that Jesus would come through.

We can start with Noah, his sons and the preservation of their DNA in the Ark to protect the bloodline. We will go into deeper detail about Noah later. Then we can go to Abraham marrying his half-sister Sarah. Or how about the miracle of Sarah giving birth at a seemingly impossible age to Isaac? Then we have Jacob laboring for 14 years for the desired ground to plant seed, before bringing forth his 12 sons and the beginning of the 12 tribes of Israel. Joseph, one of the younger sons of Jacob was not mentioned in the genealogy of Jesus because of who he married. How about Judah preserving the bloodline as he was tricked into planting his seed into his deceased son's wife, Tamar (Thamar), as she disguised herself as a prostitute?

Originally Tamar was married to Judah's son, Er. After Er's death, Tamar was married to another one of Judah's son, Omar, until he too, died. By law and custom, Tamar should have been given to Judah's next surviving son, Shelah. Judah reneged on his obligation to Tamar, so she disguised herself as a harlot to secure her rights, and became the mother of Judah's twin sons, Perez and Zerah in Genesis 38. She is the only woman recorded in the ancestral line of Jesus; this still raises some eyebrows (see Matthew 1 and Luke 3). Tamar had twins; Perez (Phares and Zerah (Zara). Another surprising fact is how Jesus came through the bloodline of David by his son Nathan, and not Solomon. Solomon turned away from God by serving other gods.

"But king Solomon loved many strange women, together with the daughter of Pharaoh, women of the Moabites, Ammonites, Edomites, Zidonians, and Hittites: of the nations concerning which the Lord said unto the children of Israel, Ye shall not go into the them, neither shall they come in unto you: for surely they will turn away your heart after their gods: Solomon clave unto these in love. And he had seven hundred wives, princesses, and three hundred concubines: and his wives turned his heart. For it came to pass, when Solomon was old, that his wives turned away his heart after other gods: and his heart was not perfect with the Lord his God, as was the heart of David his father. For Solomon went after Ashtoreth the goddess of the Zidonians, and after Milcom the abomination of the Ammonites. And Solomon did evil in the sight of the Lord, and went not fully after the Lord, as did David his father. Then did Solomon build an high place for Chemosh, the abomination of Moab, in the hill that is before Jerusalem,

and for Molech, the abomination of the children of Ammon. And likewise, did he for all his strange wives, which burnt incense and sacrificed unto their gods." 1 Kings 11: 1-8.

Solomon allowed his ungodly lust to drive him to marry, outlandish women with contaminated bloodlines to take him out of Jesus' lineage. A symbolic lineage of bloodline, is a bond and can also be called a brotherhood.

A brotherhood defines the bond Satan and the fallen angels forged together as a result of that Old Nacash's/ Satan's castration in the Garden of Eden. *"The brotherhood of the snake has been the world's most powerful tool for preserving mankind's status as a spiritually ignorant creature of toil throughout history, during all of that time, and continuing today. The Brotherhood and its network of organizations have remained intimately tied to the UFO phenomenon." - ."* –The gods of Eden. P.56.

8

The Brotherhood Oath

The word brotherhood is a fraternity or a brother from the womb. In order, to get back at God, Satan continued, in his attempt to infiltrate the pure DNA of which Jesus, the son of God, would have been born. Satan relied on his brother-hood or his frat brothers and was behind the whole debacle that occurred in Genesis chapter 6. I believe since he was now, incapable of any means of reproduction of human DNA, he convinced the Watchers in heaven to focus their attention on how beautiful the sons of Adam were. He convinced them to come down and take them as wives and plant seed into these women. The word oath means something sworn, a declaration, or a promise.

The book of the Secrets of the Book of Enoch gives us clear insight into what exactly took place concerning this brotherhood oath.

"And the Angels, the children of heaven, saw and lusted after them, and said to one another, come, let us choose us wives from among the children of men and beget us children. And Semjaza who was their leader, said unto them: I fear ye will not in deed agree to do this deed, and I alone shall have to pay the penalty of the great sin. And they all answered him and said let us all <u>swear an oath</u> and find ourselves by <u>mutual imprecations</u> not to abandon

this plan but to do this thing. The in swear they all together and bound themselves by mutual imprecations upon it. And they were in all 200; who descended in the days of Jared (to come, down) on the summit of Mount Hermon and they called it Mount Hermon because they had sworn and bound themselves by mutual imprecations upon it."
- (The Secrets of the Book of Enoch 1:6). Imprecations means evil, or curse.

I will go over more detail about these oaths that can bring curses from bloodlines to DNA. But first let's explore these secrets that the Book of Enoch mentions that was revealed to men. The book of Enoch explains further, *"And they taught them charms and enchantments, and the cutting roots, and made them acquainted with plants... and Azazel taught man to make swords, and knives, and shields, and breastplates, and made known to do the metals of the earth and the art of working them, and bracelets, and ornaments, and the use of antimony (used for paints, glass and pottery. Egyptians used it for black eye make-up.), And the beautifying of the eyelids, and all kinds of costly stones, and all coloring tinctures. And there are rules much godlessness, and they committed fornication, and they were led astray and became corrupt in all their ways...Thou seest what Azazel hath done, who had taught all unrighteousness on earth and revealed the internal secrets which were reserved in heaven, which made were striving to learn."*

We must remember when the Bible says that, *"men began to call upon the name of the Lord,"* I believe it is talking about another lord, Baal, not our Lord and Savior and Master. Howbeit, Cain began the false religion of Babylon (confusion), which all sprang from the Garden and that tree of the knowledge of good and evil, who is that old Nacash/Satan himself. When their eyes (eye, 3rd eye) was opened to the sensory realm of the flesh, their spirit was closed to the realm of the spirit. The word tree means to close the eyes. It also focuses on the spine, and represents, *"The Serpent in the New Age that climbs up the pineal gland to open up your "3rd" eye to reach enlightenment spiritually."* This is a new concept that relates to spiritual consciousness recognizing self as a "god." As opposed to recognizing the one and only God and denying self. Remember he told them that they will be as "gods." Notice the lowercase "g." This is a true oxymoron, because they were already made in the image of the Almighty God, and His Divine Nature.

Again, one of the meanings of the serpent is to prognosticate- *to predict or foretell according to present signs and indications., or to look to the future to manipulate.* The Hebrew word for knowledge is, *"daath,"* which sounds strikingly similar, to the word *"death."* It means cunning, ignorant, and unaware. This type of knowledge is actually ignorance! That's what the involvement with that tree produced, death, and ignorance of spiritual matters. From the root of this tree sprung forth, horoscopes, fortune-telling, mediums, psychics, Shamans, witchcraft, Ouija boards, crystal balls, reading of tea leaves, voodoo, Santeria, spiritual and palm reading, numerology, the operation through familiar spirits and many others. Every one of these practices are evil and used by the Satanic realm to pervert the power of God. They took the rejected secrets of heaven and perverted them to use them for evil, and they work.

That Old Nacash/Satan is an infiltrator and will mix

false religion with true religion. Remember he is a master of deception and would not foolishly publish his battle plan to control the world and contaminate the bloodline of Jesus.

The Nacash keeps it secret. It is probably very difficult for you to imagine that Satan's most effective battleground is most likely right within the church. Jesus made many references to a, *"generation of vipers."* (see, Matt. 3:7, 2:34, 23:33, Lk.3:7, Jn. 8:44, Acts 13:10, 1Jn.3:8). 33. Ye *serpents*, ye generation (offspring) of vipers," how can ye escape the damnation of hell?... 35. That upon you may come all the *righteous blood* shed upon the earth, from the blood of righteous *Abel* unto the blood of Zacharias...' –*Matt. 23:33,35.* In reference, to these vipers, "Abel" is mentioned. Could this be because of the association of Cain to these vipers and the serpent seed? It's true that he was speaking to the Pharisees and Sadducees, who are extremely religious and most likely had their bloodline contaminated with Cain's bloodline and the serpent seed.

The Pharisees and Sadducees were both religious sects that had their own beliefs. According to the Scofield Reference Bible, a member of the Pharisee was, *"chaber (knit together) and took an oath or obligation to remain true to the principles of Pharisaism. They were correct, moral, zealous, and self- denying, but self-righteous foremost persecutors of Jesus Christ and the objects of His unsparing denunciation."*

The Sadducees, again according to Scofield, were, *"Not strictly a sect, but rather those amongst the Jews who denied the existence of angels or other spirits, and all miracles, especially the resurrection. They were the religious rationalists of the time, and strongly entrenched in the Sanhedrin and priesthood. They are identified with no affirmative doctrine, but were deniers of the supernatural."*

The Sanhedrin was the highest judicial and ecclesiastical council or court of the ancient Jewish nation. It was similar to the supreme court of the USA, but it was restricted to Judea, and is likely the reason why it had no judicial authority over Jesus so long as He remained in Galilee. Jesus discerned their true nature, and their religious intent when He called them vipers as did John the Baptist.

A "brood of vipers, is a family of snakes, because vipers are venomous and deadly sons of serpents. The Pharisees and Sadducees carried The Nacash's DNA and were corrupt, legalistic, and hypocritical, which bore satanic qualities. That same satanic spirit is responsible for the death of Abel and Zechariah and can/will operate in some churches. Satan has his own agenda and servants.

I once again remind you that Satan has a literal seed and spiritual seed, in the same way that God does. He addressed them in their evil bloodline of that Old Nacash/Satan in Cain when John states, *"Ye are of (generation, offspring) your Father the Devil…he was a murderer from the beginning."-John 8:44 8. "…. The devil sinneth from the beginning."* 1 John 3:8. Cain murdered Abel in the *beginning (Foundation of the World)*, just like his daddy was a murderer in the World That Then Was *(See Book 1 -Demons Nephilim Angels, the World That Then Was)*.

Cain set his mission towards men calling on the name of his lord. They made oaths and sacrifices to their false gods, in the *Land of Nod (wandering)*. The Land of Nod is the place where Cain found his wife and is connected to an underground kingdom. An oath as defined in the dictionary is as *a solemn formal declaration or promise, <u>often calling on God</u> or a sacred object as witness. <u>An irreverent or blasphemous use of the name of God</u> was something held sacred. And imprecation, or a curse.*

Bloodlines can carry generational blessings and generational curses that are imbedded into everyone's DNA. Denouncing all those curses after coming to Christ to be born again, we receive the bloodline and DNA of Jesus, the Son of God is a necessity for eternal life in heaven. God told Cain in Genesis 4:11, *"And now thou art cursed from the earth, which hath opened her mouth to receive thy brother's blood from thy hand."* Demons feed and depend on curses in family bloodlines, made by the swearing of oaths to affect the health, well-being, and destiny of humans.

Dr. Henry Malone truthfully states, *"Freemasonry is widespread across the United States and around the world and is often passed down through family lines from <u>generation to generation</u>.... And has strong <u>bloodline connections</u>. The vows, oaths, and hidden rituals of freemasonry are undeniably demonic and have roots to the religions of Babylon (Cain). Masonic bibles, robes, rings, and other articles used in Masonic rituals, and other secret societies that carry <u>specific and far – reaching curses (diseases)</u> and must be destroyed."* Written in *Portals to Cleansing* by Dr. Henry Malone p. 28, 115.

We must ask ourselves what does the Bible and God say about engaging in and swearing oaths? The Bible warns against making excessive oaths. Therefore, Christians should avoid these kinds of oaths found in Freemasonry (this will be discussed in detail in the next chapter), which are far worse than the oaths warned against in the New Testament. Christians should let their yes be yes and no mean no. As a Christian we should and must take all oaths SERIOUSLY, and not get involved in any old organizations rashly or flippantly. This includes fraternities and sororities, that require an oath.

Leviticus 5:4 states, "Or if a soul swear, pronouncing with his lips to do evil, or to do good, whatsoever it be that a man shall pronounce with an oath, and it be hid from him; when he knoweth of it, then he shall be guilty in one of these." Matthew tells us in chapter 5 verses 34-37, 34. "But I say unto you, swear not at all; not by heaven; for it is God's throne: 35. Nor by the earth; for it is His footstool: neither by Jerusalem; but it is the city of the great King. 36. Neither shalt thou swear by thy head, because thou canst not make one hair white or black. 37. But that your communication be, Yea, yea; Nay, nay: for what soever is more than these cometh from evil." Finally, James chapter 5 verse 12 states, "But above all things, my brethren, swear not, not by heaven, neither by the earth, neither by any other oath: but let your yea be yea; and your nay, nay; lest ye fall into condemnation."

Cain was the leader or the forerunner of this oath -swearing, blood -sacrificing, false religion, secret society at the unction and leading of the fallen angels. The fallen angels or watchers received their unction and influence from the Nacash. This all started in Eden and continued in Egypt, Ethiopia, and in regions or the territory that is called Africa today. Swearing and keeping oaths to prosper in this world or this life, is the foundational principle of, *"The Brotherhood."*

Egyptian Pharaoh's and Priests belonged to *"The Brotherhood of the Snake,"* as can be clearly seen by their wardrobe and headdress, which depicted snakes. *"Brotherhood teachings were arranged as a step by step process. A student was required to satisfactorily complete one level of instruction before proceeding to the next one. All pupils took <u>oaths of secrecy</u> in which they swore never to reveal the teachings of a level to any person who had not yet graduated up to that level.... The teachings of the <u>Brotherhood</u> in ancient Egypt were organized into an institution known as the "Mystery Schools." "<u>Grand Master</u>" is the most common title used by <u>Brotherhood Organizations</u> to designate their top leaders. Guild members were often <u>free men freemasons</u>). Allegories, symbols, and costumes became extremely important because of their value,"* in The Gods of Eden p. 90 -93.

Only the pharaohs, priests, and a select few elite others who were allowed in the schools, took oaths and vows of secrecy of any secret wisdom and twisted spiritual knowledge they acquired. Before moving to the next level, the student was required to follow all instructions and prove his commitment to The Brotherhood before promoting to a higher level or degree.

The higher members of The Brotherhood taught symbols with secret meanings, and images used as a hidden secret language for those who were spiritually enlightened to be able to discern the secret codes. By doing this, it would make the elite Brotherhood look spiritually knowledgeable to those who were brothers of The Brotherhood. One of the many occult groups that claim to have hidden knowledge, is the mystical Rosicrucians.

Rosicrucianism is one of the mystical systems which arose out of The Brotherhood's teachings. Anything that is a mystery, is also supposed to be kept a secret, by its members.

Rosicrucianism according to Wikipedia, *"Holds a doctrine of theology built on esoteric truths of the ancient past, which, concealed from the average man, provide insight into nature, the physical universe and the spiritual realm."* It is symbolized by the Rosy Cross or Rose cross (incidentally all crosses are not of God). Christian Rosenkrauz is the founder of the paternity of the Rose Cross.

Rosenkrauz was born in 1378 in Germany and learned Arabic and was able to translate a secret book, the *Liber M,* into Latin. It is said that in Germany three monks from his old monastery came and joined him and became his disciples. They made secret oaths and pledges to keep secret everything that he taught them and all that they learned. There is an American Rosicrucian order that is headquartered in Quakertown, Pennsylvania, called the *Fraternity of the Rosy Cross.* They published a pamphlet called the *Fama Frateritis* also known as the *"Noted Fraternity"* or *"Famous Brotherhood."* It was printed in 1615 AD and invited readers to join the movement of *The Brotherhood.*

"Dr. Ashmole, a member of this Fraternity (Rosicrucian), is revered by Masons as one of the founders of the first Grand Lodge in London."- The Secret Teachings of All

Ages, Manly P. Hall, 1928, p.139. The Rosicrucians were a secret society guided by superstition and occult practices.

Dr. Gerard Encausse *("Papus")* wrote in his book, *"Tarot of the Benjamins,"* that, *"We must not forget that the Rosicrucians were the initiators of Leibnitz, and the <u>founders of actual Freemasonry</u> through Ashmole."* This leads us to the upcoming chapter and one of the most controversial of the secret societies, the Freemasons.

"The very word "secrecy" is repugnant
in a free and open society; and we are as people
inherently and historically opposed to secret societies,
to secret oaths and to secret proceedings...Our way of
life is under attack. Those who make themselves our
enemy are advancing around the globe... no war ever
posed a greater threat to our security...... Its (secret
societies system) preparations are concealed, not
published. Its mistakes are buried,
not headlined. Its dissenters
are silenced, not praised.
No rumor is printed, nor secret revealed."

President John F. Kennedy,
Waldorf-Astoria Hotel, New York City
April 27, 1961

9.

Freemasonry & Other Secret Societies 1

A secret society is an organization that requires its members, who are sworn to secrecy, to conceal certain activities, such as its rites of initiation, from outsiders. Keep in mind the definition for the word occult (a cult) is, relating to or dealing with supernatural influences, agencies, or phenomena, available only to the initiate; secret. To conceal, cover, or keep secret.

There are many *secret societies*, but I want to point out the main ones. We will focus most of our subject matter on Freemasonry, but here's a short list of some of the top-secret societies, today. One of the top ones is the *Order of Skull and Bones*. The *Order of Skull and Bones*, is a Yale University society, and was originally known as the brotherhood of death. It is one of the oldest student secret societies in the United States *(see my Book D.N.A. for more on the Skull and Skeleton)*.

It was founded in 1832 and only a select few could become members. To this day the society uses Masonic rituals and meet two times a week in the building they call the *"Tomb."* Both of the George Bush president's, son and father were staying members of the Skull and Bones society and many other members have gone on to reach fame, riches, and fortune. I have discussed the *Rosicrucians* and I will discuss further detail about *Freemasonry*, but the next secret society is the *Ordo Templi Orientis* or the *O.T.O.*

The *O.T.O.* is based on an initiatory system with a series of degrees ceremonies. It requires you to ceremonially give your life over to it, for fame and success. This organization was modeled after masonry but was led by one of the evillest men to ever lived on the face of this earth. His name is *Aleister Crowley*. He nicknamed himself *"666"* and the *"Great Beast."*

Aleister Crowley, one of the most famous masters of the occult, was secretly the father of Barbara Pierce Bush, and grandfather of George W. Bush and Jed Bush according to the internet. Chuck Klosterman talks about Crowley in one of his books.

Charles "Chuck" Klosterman, an American author and essayist, who has written over ten books that focuses on American popular culture, mentions Aleister Crowley in one of his books, I Wear the Black Hat.

Crowley implemented principles of his religious system called the *Law of Thelema,* and it was based on the one law: *"Do what thou wilt."* This goes completely against God's will being done in our lives as His children. He drew a picture of a being or evil spirit, that he named *"Lam."* This was a fallen spirit being from whom he received his knowledge. The photo of "Lam" bears a striking resemblance to the big- headed modern day aliens of today. This was done in the 1940's.

Channeling is an ancient occult practice used to contact demons, way before the 1940's. Crowley learned this from 33rd degree Freemason and French magician Eliphas Levi created a special circle with a hexagram in the middle of the floor, with four corners of magic. With a picture of the Baphomet on the wall, Eliphas conjured up the demon Apollonius into this dimension, all the while with a _spell book_ in his hand. In the Masonic book, *"The Spirit of Masonry,"* which was published in 1975. We are told, *"Masons know the way of gaining an understanding of Abrac."* Abrac is a type of magic, and where we get the term *Abracadabra."* Crowley was an avid disciple of magic.

To become a member of Crowley's occult, a person had to go through degrees of initiations that were very similar to the initiations of Cain. Cain built a city, *"Enoch"* and named his *first-born* son, Enoch, which means to initiate. Enoch was dedicated to, initiated in, and taught the teachings of Babylon. Crowley believed in the same spirits that Cain worshiped, contacted, and channeled to in his occult.

Crowley created a *"Mass"* for the *OTO*, the *"Gnostic Mass."* It teaches that to become famous you must become a member of or pass through this secret order. He promoted and practiced the ritual of channeling spirits of many Egyptian gods and invoking the presence of demons and the devil as well. He practiced and taught child molestation for power. He taught how to invoke and *channel Satan and demons, (Black, Sex) magic, spells and backwards messages.*

They even have rituals involving virgin priestesses (like Eve). There it is again sex, just like in the Garden of Eden. He is responsible for the musical influences of the many artists that are beloved around the world, today.

The Bible clearly, specifically, and often speaks against consulting (channeling) or seeking after *familiar spirits* (see *Lev. 19:31, 20:6, 27, Deut. 18:11, 1 Sam. 28:3-9, 1 Chron.10:13, 2 Chron. 33:6, Isa. 8:19, 19:3, 29:4).* The channeling of the old Nephilim, demonic spirits are the real artists and composers behind most of the music of the past, and most contemporary genres today. The list includes Michael Jackson, Prince, The Beatles, Led Zeppelin, and many, many, more.

The *Bilderberg Meeting or group* is different from the others because there is no official membership. The name is associated with the group of people who are extremely influential, prominent people, top bankers, and political figures, who congregate every year secretly with the security of the military, and the U.S. government. There are conference meetings held in secret locations around the world, and it is by invitation only. *Prince Bernard of the House of Orange in the Netherlands,* member of *The Nazi Secret Service,* and *Chairman of Shell Oil,* founded the international *"Bilderberg "* meetings.

The first meeting took place in 1954 at the *Hotel Bilderberg* in the Netherlands. Unfortunately, the contents of the meetings are secret, the attendees pledge by swearing to a secret oath, not to divulge any of the information that was disseminated or discussed.

Another secret society is *The Hermetic Order of The Golden Dawn.* Dr. William Robert Woodman, William Wynn Westcott, and Samuel Liddell Macgregor Mathers created this secret order. All three of these men were Freemasons. This is widely considered to be a forerunner to the *O.T.O.* in many occult groups. *The Golden Dawn* beliefs are taken from Christian mysticism, Kabbalah,

Hermeticism; the religion of ancient Egypt, Freemasonry, Alchemy, Theosophy, and Magic. They produced documents that contained magic rituals.

Mathers was obsessed with Black Magic and connected closely to Crowley. Crowley hated Christians and Christianity. He saw himself as the new Messiah of a new religion. Jesus warned us in His word that there would be many *false Christs* in the lasts days. Another secret society is *The Knights Templar.*

The Knights Templar or *Templar Knights* is a secret society that began as an extension or branch of *The Brotherhood.* They had a tradition of practicing mysticism and used Brotherhood titles, like, *"Grand Master,"* and *"Worshipful Master."* They are different than and are not connected to the religious military group formed in the 12th-century, the original *Knights Templar. They* do use and borrow mediaeval symbols.

The criteria for becoming a member of this group is that you already must be a *Christian Master Mason.* Certain degrees and orders are of a mediaeval pattern and symmetry. A good way to describe these are *"commemorative orders"* or *"degrees."* Many of the rites or degrees of Freemasonry have been directly influenced by the Templar.

The secret society that is the most notorious and accepted in society, especially among Christians is *Freemasonry. Freemasonry* is the name of one of the largest and oldest fraternal organizations in the world. It's a secret society that originated from the root of serpent *brotherhood* and sun worship. Freemasonry involves swearing oaths, making vows and pledges, and it is under the guise of promoting brotherhood and morality. Anyone in any religious position of authority can be persuaded, and even encouraged to join the Masons. This is where the term that you see so often today, *Coexist*, comes from.

There are symbols that form the word *COEXIST.* Every letter has a symbol that represents a system or a thought. It consists of; The crescent and star are for *Islam; the pentacle for Wicca; the relativity formula for Science; the star of David for Judaism; the karma wheel dotting the i for Buddhism; the Tao symbol for Taoism; the cross for Christianity;* unfortunately (false) *Christianity.*

This is a New World Order principle in bringing all the religions into agreement as one with many gods. *Symbolism* is very important in secret societies because of the deeper spiritual content behind it. *Freemasonry* may be the best at using it.

Freemasonry has been defined as, *"a system of morality veiled in allegory and illustrated by symbols." (Satan's Angels Exposed, p. 134, Salem Kirk).* I want you to really pay attention to this next quote from one of the Master Masons, Manly P. Hall. *"Symbolism is the language of the mysteries...By symbols men have ever sought to communicate to each other those thoughts which transcend the limitations of language......In a single figure a symbol may both reveal and conceal, while the ignorant to the figure remains inscrutable." - (The Secret Teachings of All Ages, p.20, Manly P. Hall).*

As a matter of fact, Albert Pike alludes to *Freemasonry* as a religion. Therefore, a Christian or follower of Jesus Christ, should not be a follower of another religion, especially if it is not in line with the Word of God. Now, back to the symbolism in *Freemasonry.*

The primary symbol in Freemasonry is the Masonic

compass and the T-square. The Masonic symbol of the compass and the T-square represents movement toward perfection and a balance between the spiritual and physical, and the sons of God and daughters of men. They believe in building a new man and a New World Order. The compass and t- square also represents sex, as with a penis and a vagina, and a fusion of genders. This all came from that *Old Nacash/Satan* in the garden.

What does the Bible say about the compass and the T-Square? *"The carpenter stretcheth out his rule: he marketh it out with a line: He fitteth it with planes, and he marketh it out with a compass, and maketh it after the figure of a man, according to the beauty of a man; that it may remain in the house."* – Isaiah 44:13. The compass and T-square represents man, and not God. The letter "g" in the middle of the symbol has several meanings. god (not our God, *their god is Lucifer), geometry, goddess, good* and *evil,* and *gnosis.*

An atheist can't become a member because you must believe in something so that they can manipulate, and mold you. They even wear lamb-skin aprons to symbolize what happened with Adam and Eve in the Garden. It is a gift of Freemasonry to a candidate and buried with the candidate at the end of his life.

It is a badge of a Mason. They would like their secret sins to stay covered, so to speak. There is even a Masonic Bible. Masons don't believe in the God of the Bible, despite what they profess openly. There is even a secret handshake that is called, *"TubalCain." TubalCain* is one of Cain's great, great, great, great grandsons.

This all came from Cain's cursed bloodline. A constitution (oath) was made to keep these curses going throughout the bloodline, even to this day. Connection, brotherhood, and membership to any secret societies, especially

Freemasonry can bring sickness, and diseases into a person's bloodline, until it is renounced. It does not matter how far back in the bloodline that the connection was made.

It must be renounced and broken by the blood of Jesus Christ, to severe the generational, DNA, by faith. *"Freemasonry is widespread across the United States and around the world and is often passed down family lines from generation to generation. It's hidden rituals of initiation and occult degrees are totally against God's word. Whether you or your ancestors have been Masons, Shriners, Knight of Columbus, Knights Templars or members of any other ungodly secret societies, the rings, regalia, books and objects used in the ceremonies must be destroyed. Recently I heard the story of a woman ... her grandfather had been a Mason. He had given her some of his ceremonial items. She had framed and put them on one of the walls in her home. When the occult roots of masonry were told to her and the suggestion of the items being removed she said, "I'll die first before I get rid of those." .... two weeks later doctors discovered that she had cancer. I prayed for her healing and told her to repent, go home and burn the objects. She did. Within a week her doctors had miraculous news the cancer was totally gone."* (Portals to Cleansing, p.28, 29, Dr. Henry Malone).

10.
Freemasonry & Secret Societies (2) The Church

Before Freemasonry came to America, it began with Cain's bloodline, the seed of that *Old Nacash/Satan*. It all started with Cain's descendants, the cities that they built and the rituals that they established.

"A Masonic constitution dated 1701 refers to Genesis 4:16- 24. From the line of Cain (through Methusael) was born Lamech (Genesis 4:18). From Lamech's marriage to two wives (Adah and Zillah) came four children: Adah was born Jabal and Jubal... and to Zillah was born Tubalcain and a daughter, Naamah (Genesis 4:20-22). The Masonic Constitution relates that these four discovered the major crafts of the world (mathematics, stonemasonry, ironwork and weaving) from two pillars of stone. The one stone called Latarus and the other Marbell. According to Freemason symbolism Enoch (son of Cain), erected the two pillars of stone." (Satan's Angels Exposed, p, 142, 143, Salem Kirk).

So now you can see the origin of the bloodline Constitution and the inception into Masonry. Moses tells us in Genesis 4:17 that Cain built a city, and called it, *Enoch,* after his son. It was in Enoch that he began his Babylonian teachings, because Enoch means to initiate, dedicate, and teach.

In 1717, four fraternal lodges united under the grand Lodge of England, incidentally Masons meet in lodges. As we examine the nature of the degrees of initiations, an important note, as the lodges spread quickly, there were many then and are still many famous members, including presidents. A few well-known members were: *Benjamin Franklin, George Washington, Frederick the Great of Prussia, and every US president* whose picture is on money, and many more. Even up to active Masons of today; musicians, singers, actors, rappers, politicians, notable leaders, and just about most if not all, of the famous people in the world.

According to Salem Kirk, as a Mason joins, he joins a *Blue Lodge* which holds 3 degrees: *Entered Apprentice, Fellowcraft,* and *Master Mason.* Apparently, the participation in secret ceremonies can elevate the Mason to advance in degrees.

There are many interconnected affiliated organizations with *Freemasonry* such as: the Scottish Rite, the York Rite, Mystic Shrines, and many fraternities and sororities, which I will discuss shortly.

It has been said, that if you reveal the secrets you have your tongue cut out. The higher the level or degree, one also attains revelation knowledge, especially the 32nd and 33rd degree, and are made to spit on a cross and do homosexual acts. Then it is revealed to you that you are serving the god of this world, Lucifer or Satan, and his rulers of the darkness of this world, and spiritual wickedness in high places. Ephesians 6:12.

Of course, any time a faction of people is privileged to have something, then another faction of people long for it. This is the same principle of temptation that the old Nacash/Satan used in the Garden of Eden.

In the Garden of Eden, Adam and Eve were living in paradise, in a state of bliss or ultimate happiness, until Satan tempted them with his deceitful lies. They had everything. Satan told them that their eyes would be opened to the spiritual realm and they would become gods, knowing good and evil.

Sadly, many African-Americans wanted what they didn't have and sought to obtain their own faction of Freemasonry, under the, *"Master Masons."*

In 1904, the first African -American Greek Secret Society was formed inPhiladelphia, by Dr. Henry Minton, who also owned the first Black drug store in the United States, with five of his colleagues. Minton wanted to create a Black secret society based on the beliefs, and customs of the Skull and Bones also known as, the *Brotherhood of Death*. Around the same time as the founding of the *Boulé,* we find the founding of the NAACP and the Urban League. *The Boule,* (an acronym for Sigma Pi Phi) and pronounced "boo-lay"), was formed to bring together a select group of educated Black men and women.

They are called archons (lords, masters) chosen by the US government to run Black neighbor-hoods. There are many members of *The Boule* today, but of course they keep it a *secret,* because it is a *secret society.*

Boule means *"advisors to the king,"* and has the Sphinx (1/3woman, 1/3 eagle, 1/3 lion) as their logo. Boule members take a sworn oath. The members of this group are Black, rich, and famous, and are funneled and recruited from their brother-hood and sisterhood affiliations, otherwise known as fraternities and sororities. There is a Boule membership book with some very interesting and surprising names.

Recruitment for Black secret societies are done through fraternities, and sororities. I will come back to *The Boule, Prince Hall Freemasonry* and the Church, after I reveal the truth about fraternities and sororities, which are <u>Greek Lettered Organizations</u> *(G.L.O. 's)*. There is even a female faction of Freemasonry known as the Eastern Stars.

My mom told me that she used to be a member of the Eastern Stars in Los Angeles in the 1960's. She said they met on Saturdays in a hall on Arlington Blvd. There were girls between the ages of 11 and 20 who attended the meetings. She joined just to have something to do and to get away from home.

They had fund raisers to pay their way to a national convention in Fresno, California during the summer when school was out. The money paid for a chartered bus, food, and their stay at the hotel in Fresno. She remembered the line of March. All the girls had to wear white dresses and white shoes. Each charter had to compete in the line-of-March. The winner, won a scholarship for the oldest girl in the charter. At the convention were both men and women.

The men wore, "a funny looking, pointed hats with tassels (fez) and an embroidered blazer." The older women were dressed in their best evening gowns. The men were the judges of the charter who did the best line-of-March. There was a *Princess Ingrid* and a *Princess Geraldine*, who represented the charters. Her charter won some money, but she doesn't remember how much.

My mom said later, after she became a Christian, she

wanted to get filled with the Holy Spirit, but something was hindering her. She had to denounce her involvement in the Eastern Stars before being filled. God is a jealous God. Moses said, *"Thou shalt not bow down thyself to them, (graven images) nor serve them: for I the Lord thy God am a jealous God..."* Exodus 20:5. My mom said, *"There was some bowing and homage shown to the men in the Eastern Stars."* She found out about the *Eastern Stars* from the church she attended.

Now, the *Order of the Eastern Stars* is the world's largest fraternal organization to which both men and woman may join. It is open to all people of faiths. It gives support to young people who will be attending a college, university or community college.

Freemasonry, some fraternities and sororities have a connection with occultism. Occultism is done and practiced in secret. In freemasonry there are special handshakes, secret code words and symbolism. G.L.O.'s serve and worship false Greek gods and goddesses and engage in traditional freemason rituals, unwittingly.

These fraternities and sororities engage in idolatry and give devotion, agreement and service to these false gods. They pay homage to Thor, Qetesh, Minerva or Athena, Thoth, Atlas, Anubis, Bastet, and Apollo. The symbols of these gods and goddesses are openly hidden in their logos and flashed in their hand signs.

The very first commandment in Exodus chapter 20 is *"Thou shalt have no other gods before me."* They are required to constantly repeat oaths, rituals, pledges, hand signs or symbols and dances like stepping, which is considered paying respect and honor to whichever god is over that fraternity or sorority.

The Boule and *Freemasonry* specifically, recruit members from these G.L.O.'s through parties, bonding and community gatherings. When they join, they must engage in deplorable, sick hazing occult rituals to show their allegiance. A Christian should never join any of these organizations, but regrettably, recruitment is not only done in G.L.O.'s but also in the body of Christ, a lot of churches that profess to be Christians.

Prince Hall is recognized as the father of Black *Freemasonry,* who helped to incorporate recruiting in the church or Body of Christ. *Freemasonry* was only for white men. So, to start another sub faction of Freemasonry, white masons called on Prince Hall under the permission and guise of the Skull, and Bones to begin Prince Hall Freemasonry in Philadelphia. It is a Freemason group for Black people. One of his first members, Richard Allen, was the founder of the first A.M.E. (African Methodist Episcopal Church and the treasurer for Prince Hall Freemasonry).

Prince Hall and Richard Allen worked together to use the A.M.E. church to recruit and influence members to join Prince Hall Freemasonry. There are many Christian churches that still practice recruiting for Freemasonry today.

Freemasonry's origin is not Christian but based on paganism. Masons may endeavor to do good works but a believer in Christ cannot be a member of any secret society! They are either going to be faithful to one and compromise the other, depending on what they are required to do and say. There are many pastors and preachers who are esteemed members of Freemasonry. Many of the televangelists that you see on television today are associated with Freemasonry.

You cannot serve two masters. Freemasonry allows all religions, with the coexist factor, with Lucifer as their god. But keep in mind this is all done in secret. In Matthew 7:22, 23 Jesus says, 22. *"Many will say to me in that day, Lord, Lord, have we not <u>prophesied in thy name</u>? And in <u>thy name cast out devils</u>? And in thy name done many wonderful works? 23. And then I will say unto them, <u>I never knew you;</u> depart from me, ye that work iniquity."*

In an anonymous survey taken in some of the highly esteemed Christian church affiliations, it was discovered that over 43,000 pastors/ministers were initiated into becoming Freemasons from every denomination. An extremely high percentage of mega-churches and pastors are Masons. When asked if the issue of *Freemasonry* ever caused a problem in the churches/associations, majority of each group responded that their churches /associations had never dealt with *Freemasonry*. Of those responding pastors, ministers of education, directors of missions, deacons, elders, chairman, and church clerks were or had been Masonic or Eastern Star members. Ask your Pastors if he/she is a Freemason and ask about *Freemasonry*. If they are members, then you need to leave that church immediately.

Probably the greatest, modern day revivalist of all time, Charles G. Finney had some critical observations and revelations on *Freemasonry* and Christianity. Finney probably one of the greatest of the 19th-century evangelists, left Freemasonry when he acknowledged Christ as his Savior and the Lord of his life, and before being filled with the Holy Spirit. He wrote a book entitled, *Freemasonry* in 1835.

One of the things he said was that Masons are in the

pulpit, in leadership positions, and sitting in church pews. He also stated, *"While masonry was the secret, the church had no light, and no responsibility revealing it... Since God did not require the church to bear any testimony on the subject, as long as masonry was secret. Freemasonry is now revealed. It is no longer a secret from any who wishes to be informed."* He also said, *"Surely, if Masons really understood what masonry is, no Christian Mason would think himself to remain at liberty to remain another day a member of the fraternity. It is as plain as possible that a man knowing what it is and embrace it in his heart, cannot be a Christian man. To say he can is to belittle the very nature of Christianity."*

Our loyalty as Christians should only be to Christ Jesus. It is sad that when Pastors supposedly "unveil" the truth behind fraternities, sororities, and other secret societies that they leave out the church. It is on full display for those that have eyes to see their hand signs, ministry symbols, and its teachings. It's no longer hidden, it's in plain sight! There is a plethora of famous preachers who are Freemasons and see nothing wrong with it, because they declare that they are Freemasons for Jesus. It would shock you if I showed you a list of the many familiar preachers that are Freemasons and Illuminati members. If you say to yourself their gift is still working. The gifts and callings of God are irrevocable. God will judge them! Pray and ask the Holy Spirit to reveal to you if your Pastor is involved in Freemasonry? There is another secret society connected with Freemasonry, ***"The Illuminati."***

11.

ILLUMINATI
AND
THE ALL- SEEING EYE

Illuminati comes from the root word *"illuminate."* It basically means to give light or one who is enlightened in mind and spirit. The Illuminati are a people defined as having and professing spiritual enlightenment and special intellectual abilities. *"In Germany and elsewhere, the brotherhood and someof its most advanced initiates had become known by a Latin name: The Bavarian Illuminati. Advancement through the Rosicrucians in degrees often resulted in admittance to the illuminati."*(Gods of Eden, p.196/197).

Remember Lucifer, (a Latin term, meaning Heylale, to shine, bright) was originally illuminated as the bright, shining clear sounding boasting son from the beginning. He was skilled in all wisdom, a beautiful, completely brilliant creation by God. Lucifer realized that he was made privy to information and revelation from God that only he knew. Remember he is able to transform himself into an angel of light.

The order of the Illuminati was founded on May 1, 1776 by Dr. Adam Weishaupt a professor of canon law at the University of Ingolstadt in Bavaria. Take notice of the date. It is the same time of America's Declaration of Independence. Novices were taken to a dimly lit room in the darkest of the night, where they learned secret signs and the password.

Weishaupt is quoted on how he lured unsuspecting people to the Illuminati. He wrote, *"These people swell our numbers and fill our treasury; get busy and make these people nibble at our bait... But do not tell them our secrets. They must be made to believe that the low degree that they have reached is the highest."* - (Satan's Angels Exposed, by Salem Kirban, p.149). He eventually infiltrated the Freemasons and created an alliance between the two organizations. Fifteen lodges of the Illuminati were established in the 13 colonies.

In the doctrine of the Illuminati, Lucifer is their God. They don't believe in Satanism, but Lucifer is their god of light. This has basis in Gnosticism because they teach that the Christian God is the God of evil.

According to Albert Pike, an intellectual genius and member of both the Illuminati and Freemasonry stated that, *"The masonic religion should be, by all of us initiates of the high degrees, maintained in the purity of the Luciferian Doctrine."* (p. 161, Satan's Angels Exposed, by Salem Kirban).

The Illuminati takes orders from the fallen angels who rule over secret societies through the serpent seed, as the rulers of darkness of this world. According to Felix Frankfurter, a US Supreme Court Justice, during the FDR administration, *"The real rulers in Washington are invisible and exercise power from behind-the-scenes."* This statement is an inference towards aliens being in control. There are 13 parent families with uncontaminated bloodlines that rule the Illuminati.

The Illuminati royal bloodlines start with the top families: Rothschild, Astor, Bundy, Collins, DuPont, Freeman, Kennedy, Li, Onassis, Rockefeller, Disney (one of the reasons why Disneyworld has people under a spell), Russell, Van Duyne, Merovingian, and Reynolds. Yes! Disney sends subtle occult and satanic messages through his cartoons, movies, and amusement parks. It is all designed to put children in a trance and slip in suggestions of the occult before their eyes.

You should be careful what you believe when it comes to the media, because the Illuminati controls every facet of the media. The Illuminati also controls sports, television, electronics, the internet, the movie industry, and even religion. The heavy hitters, or major celebrities, athletes, politicians, world and local leaders, major business corporations, and stars are members of and controlled by the Illuminati. I mean, seriously, wouldn't you have to question anyone who has ever received a *"star"* on the *Hollywood Walk of Fame?"* The Illuminati rewards their own, so there must be a connection. The Illuminati is behind the LGBTQ (Lesbian, gay, bisexual, transgendered, and queer (or questioning) movement because their founder Lucifer engaged in transgenderism, which all began in the Garden of Eden.

Right before the sexual activity began in the Garden and during the Nacash's verbal seduction, he spoke a key phrase in Genesis 3:5, *"...then your eyes shall be opened.."* In Freemasonry the number 33 is significant. One of the highest degrees a freemason can receive is the 33rd degree. It is fitting that the word _eyes_, is the 33rd word spoken to

Eve by the Nacash KJV). The word eyes or "eye" as in 3rd eye, or the <u>All-Seeing Eye</u>, represents enlightenment, and opens the door to New Age, Occult, and Mysticism.

In the New Age they believe that the serpent climbs up the spine and the pineal gland, in order to open up, the 3rd eye to reach enlightenment spiritually. The Illuminati adopted the All-Seeing Eye symbol from their inception.

It is easy to spot, the supposed incognito, All-Seeing Eye. It is on the back of the dollar bill as a representation of Nimrod and the Tower of Babel. Freemasons are believers in Nimrod as the Great Architect of The Universe. It is also seen in the Meditation room of the United Nations in New York. It is a symbol made famous by Aleister Crowley. They say The Great Seal is the All –Seeing Eye of god. However, the words underneath the pyramid in Latin read, "(Novus Ordo Seclorum) meaning, *"New Secular or World Order."*

The words in Latin above the Great Seal read, (Annuit Coeptis) meaning, *"Announcing the Birth."* If you put them together it states, *"Announcing the Birth of The New World Order."* The cornerstone is missing from the top of the pyramid. The All -Seeing Eye has become the cornerstone. It supplants the cornerstone, which is Jesus Christ. Christ's importance is removed. According to Ephesians 2:20, *"Jesus Christ Himself...the chief corner stone.* Mark 12 :10 and Luke 20:17 describes Him as, *"The Stone which the builders rejected."* Jesus has been rejected on the US dollars.

Also, on the dollar bill is Shiva or Kali the Hindu god of destruction, with several arms, is sitting in the yoga position with a mark on the forehead symbolizing the third eye. This false god represents death, darkness, the god of yoga and transcendental meditation. It teaches you to tap into self and the third eye that you have inside. Shiva is a fallen angel according to Revelation 9:11, *"And they had a king over them, which is the angel of the bottomless pit, his name in Hebrew is Abaddon, but in Greek his name is Apollyon."* I don't think that it is a coincidence that this verse is located in Revelation 9:11. We use 9-1-1 to call for help during an emergency. Abaddon and devils like it. They have caused a lot of emergencies, the Twin Towers in New York, the destruction and death on September 11, 2001 (9-11).

An eye, which it is commonly called, is considered mind control or MK ultra is what they call it. It's like being under a trance or a spell, and under the control of the spirit sending the trance or spell. It is a form of magic and enchantment used to control its subject through symbols such as the All –Seeing Eye. *"Many mystical teachings are still taught today in the <u>Jewish Kabbalah</u>: a secret religious philosophy of Jewish rabbis. The Kabbalah continues to utilize a complex array of <u>mystical symbols</u>. Israel's national logo has been a <u>Brotherhood</u> symbol for thousands of years."* - The Gods of Eden p.79.

The hexagram on Israel's flag is not a star. It is a hexagram; a symbol of the occult promoted by the Rothschilds when they helped to make Israel become a nation in 1948. The Jewish people say it is the Star of David, but David never had a star. It is the seal of Solomon. It is where the term "put a hex" came from. A hexagram calls forth demons and establishes a curse. In other words, to put a curse on someone.

In the Illuminati, celebrities or stars, supposedly are illuminated, because of their gifts, talents, and abilities. The kind of stars that he is referring to is found in acts chapter 7 verse 43, *"Yea, you take up the tabernacle of Moloch of Moloch, and the <u>star</u> (constellation: single or artificial star) of your God Remphan, figures which you made to worship them: and I will carry you beyond Babylon."*

If you pay close attention to celebrities, you will always know their allegiance, because they place the 666- okay sign, around the eye symbolizing the All-Seeing third eye. The Illuminati is against Christianity and serves Satan as their god whom they called Lucifer. Lucifer is their god of of light. The Illuminati has been behind World Wars I and II and will cause World War III. The Antichrist will be in league with the Illuminati and put forth his plan during the seven-year tribulation period. The Illuminati-Freemasonry is in all secret societies and evil political movements are controlled by Satan. This all originated from the Garden of Eden.

Of course, I believe everyone has a third eye. Once you give your life to Jesus and make Him your Lord, you relinquish control and ownership of your light (or third eye) to Him. This could be why traditionally hands are laid on the forehead where the third eye is located. When you open your spirit to illumination and light to anything but the true living God, you become vulnerable to attacks and mind control. Matthew 6:22-24 says, *"the <u>light</u> of the body is the <u>eye:</u> if therefore thine eye be <u>single (clear),</u> thy whole body shall be <u>full of light.</u> 23. But if thine eye be <u>evil,</u> thy whole body shall be <u>full of darkness.</u> If therefore the light that is in the be darkness, how great is that darkness! 24. No man can serve two masters: for either he will hate the one and love the other: or else he will hold to the one and despise the other. Ye cannot serve God and mammon."*

So, this tells us that the light that the Illuminati receives from the All-Seeing third eye is dark light, false light, evil. And it is all centered around money, which is why in the very next verse Matthew tells us not to take thought for our life or worry about what we should eat or put on, because if we trust in Jesus he will provide for us. Remember that the *Tree of Life* represents Jesus (The Anointed), and true Light.

The tree of knowledge of good and evil represents darkness, false (dark) light, and money. Only if we protect our spirits and do not open ourselves up to great darkness but inviting spirits to come in and dim or extinguish the light God has given us. Be careful what you dabble in. When we do this, we give devils the right to afflict, torment, and negatively affect us. And it can come to torcher us at any time especially when we are sleeping.

12.

Incubus and Succubus

That Old Nacash likes to attack us when we are sleeping, especially when we have knowingly or unknowingly opened the door. Maybe people believe that Christians cannot be possessed by demons. Well I did not believe that. I believe whatever you open yourself up to has the ability to possess you. If you play with Ouija boards and crystal balls and go to psychics, then of course; you have opened yourself up for demonic attack and possession. This is where the incubus and succubus spirit come into play. First, let's back up and talk about this spirit.

It is believed by many that Lilith was Adam's first wife. Even though we are not directly told this in the Bible, especially in the book of Genesis. But the possibility is intriguing based on certain portions of scripture.

If you do a thorough study in the book of Genesis, you will ask yourself how to find out why there were no other people on the planet? It stands to reason that there were people on the planet before God made Adam and Eve and placed them in the outside of the *Garden* of Eden. Remember earlier we talked about those trees representing people in the Garden of Eden. Look at Adam's response that, *"This is now bone of my bones, and flesh of my flesh: she shall be called woman, because she was taken out of man.*" – Genesis 2:23. It is almost as if he is stating this *one* is from my DNA.

It seems that now this Lilith is somewhere between a human and the spirit engaging in sexual prowess to corrupt and effect men and women.

In Isaiah 34:14, 15 we are able to locate her, "14. *the wild beasts of the desert shall also meet with the wild beasts of the island, and the satire shall cry to his fellow; the screech owl (Lilith- a night spectre, winding stair (DNA) ghost), also shall rest there, and find for herself a place of rest. 15. There shall the great owl make her nest and lay, and hatch, and gather (brood over) under her shadow: there shall the vultures (fly rapidly) also be gathered, everyone with her mate. Notice the screech owl is called, "Lilith,"* a night ghost and is made from different DNA and Adam. Lilith is considered a beast.

The screech owl is referred to as herself, meaning it is a female that has wings and flies. It also broods over people with her shadow while they are sleeping. It is even believed that this Lilith is the cause of miscarriages, and crib and infant deaths while brooding and hovering over children. When it comes to DNA we know that adenine pairs with thymine and Cytosine with Guanine (A,T,G,C). A, pairs with her mate T, and C, pairs with her mate G, "*everyone with her mate*." The nucleotides pair with their mate that is the formula for God's DNA. Therefore, we know that Lilith was not made of Adam's DNA. She did not pair with him.

If this was Adam's first wife part of her punishment for leaving Adam and not being submissive to him because she felt that they were equal, and she wanted to dominate him., was the inability to conceive, bear children. Many believe it to be true of the legend of Lilith is that she wanted to be on top during sexual intercourse, and not on the bottom. She is now relegated to being a demon that steals semen and eggs from women during a dream-like state while asleep.

In Exo Vaticana, page 124 we read, *"... The incubi and succubi of Sinastri's opinion were neither evil spirits nor fallen Angels but corporeal beings created midway between humans and angels."* Basically, they are devils. These devils usually appeared in night as either a seductive demon in a male human form called, "incubi" or *"Incubus."* From this we derive the Latin term *"incubo"*, which means "to lie upon."

So, when women are asleep and think that they are dreaming about a sexual episode, it is actually happening. In Africa, they call them the night husband or the night wife.

The spirit can seduce you and rape you while you're lying right there in bed with your spouse. It is having phantasmagoric intercourse with women, or elsewhere as a sensual female presence known as *"succubi,"* which means *"to lie under."* This is summed up in excellent fashion in Exo-Vaticana, pages 126 and 127. *"The succubus collects semen from men through dream-state copulation (sexual intercourse). Some believe these entities are one of the same. The same spirit may appear as female in one instance to collect male seed, then reappear elsewhere as a male to transfer the semen into a womb. "*

How about nightmares? Have you ever had one? Why do they frighten us? The dictionary defines a nightmare as a frightening or unpleasant dream. I have been speaking about this spirit at churches and more than a half of the audience has experienced nightmares or a feeling of something getting on top of them and suffocating them where they can't even speak. Maybe it wouldn't surprise you to know that the term nightmare, actually, derives from the old English maere for a goblin or incubus. It variously referred to an evil female spirit that afflicted sleepers with a feeling of suffocation and that dreams and/ or elsewhere as a seductress causing wet dreams and young men.

From this we see that wet dreams are not natural and are not from God. Incubus when having intercourse with women begets the human fetus from his own seed. The solution is that even if the incubus gets on top of you and you cannot speak and it is trying to suffocate you, I have heard people say that just the thought of the name of Jesus will cause this devil to flee, even if you cannot utter Jesus' name at that moment. The Incubus spirit can appear male and sexually seduce males, in an attempt to release a spirit of homo-sexual confusion. The same can be done for Succubus and a female, thus releasing a lesbian spirit.

Eye witnesses have testified of seeing either a winged woman or a winged man in their bed-room on top of them. Could this be another one of the secrets from the Garden of Eden that is affecting God's children this very day?

The Incubus and Succubus spirit is active in the world today and is affluent among celebrities and musicians. The Illuminati and Secret Societies are prime candidates to promote this devil through their music, movies, and art. Deception through seduction is the tactic that that Old Nacash used in the Garden of Eden. Consider the quotes of some celebrities who admit to having sexual encounters with incubus and succubus and even enjoyed it.

Actress in Charlie's Angels star, Lucy Lu, told Us

Weekly in 1999, *"Some sort of spirit came down from God, from nowhere and made love to me..." It was sheer bliss. I felt everything. I climaxed. Then he floated away. It was almost like what might have happened to Mary. That's how it felt something came down and touched me and now it watches over me..."*

In 2004, actress, Anna Nicole Smith told *FHM* magazine, *"A ghost would crawl up my leg and have sex with me at an apartment a long time ago in Texas. I used to think it was my boyfriend, and one day I woke up and it wasn't. It was, like, a spirit and it – WOO! (miming a ghost flying from her bedsheets)- went up! I was freaked out about it, but then I was, like, well, you know what? He's never hurt me and he just gave me some amazing facts so I have no problem."* She protested that it was happening every night.

Blues Brothers and Ghostbusters star, Dan Aykroyd stated in a 2010 blogpost for *The Huffington Post that, "He felt an unseen presence in his bed."* Then in a 2013 interview with Esquire, he reported, *"cuddling with a male ghost in his bed, and thinking, I'm just going to roll over and snuggle up next to it."*

In 2012 Pop star, body glitter innovator, Kesha claimed during an interview with Ryan Seacrest that her song Supernatural was inspired by *"Having sexy time with a ghost."*

Also, in 2012 Coco Austin, model, and wife of actor/ rapper Ice -T, claimed on the talk show *Naughty by Nice, said, "I was watching TV... I was wearing a nightie and I felt something on my leg... I looked down and got freaked out. I pushed it down to watch TV, felt it again and I could see that my nightie was being pulled up. Then I felt the guy breathing in my ear."*

As we can see from these quotes, ever since the Garden and even before, secret sexual seduction has been a tactic of the enemy. If you recall in Genesis 4:1, Eve said, *"I have gotten a man from the Lord."* She thought she was referring to the Lord God. But she was actually seduced, enchanted, and put under a love spell by, that Old Nacash, who is also known as Baal. Another term for Baal is Lord or Master. In the Old Testament, Yahweh and Baal worship were unfortunately often blended together. This practice was introduced to Israel through Jezebel. Baal was the storm god or fertility/sex god. Worship of Baal involved imitative magic, the performance of sexual rituals and male and female prostitution.

Incubus and Succubus are winged corporeal human-like, creatures. The purpose of wings is *to fly,* quite simply put. The ancient deity, Baal was also *"Lord of War,"* and *"Lord of Sky."* Many titles were given to Baal by adding endings to his name. Some examples found in scripture are *Baalhazor – "Lord of the Fortresses," Baalbamoth – "Lord of the high places," and Baalzebub- "Lord of those who flit or fly."* Zebub is a Hebrew verb, which means to flit from place to place, having been popularly translated as the, *"Lord of the flies,"* it is more properly rendered, *"Lord of those things that fly."* So that Old Nacash is the prince of Baal's airspace.

The incubus is also known as the Queen of the night, which is coincidental because male and female consorts the god Baal, and the goddess Asherah or Astarte is known as the Queen of heaven. This of course leads us to Jezebel, a witch, who worshiped Baal and Astarte. Jezebel was dedicated to Baal as a baby by her Father Ethbaal from Phoenicia.

In Revelations 2:14, we are told of Jezebel, *"notwithstanding I have a few things against me, because thou sufferest (leave alone, permit,) that woman Jezebel, which calleth herself a prophetess, to teach and to seduce my servants to commit fornication, and to eat things sacrificed unto idols."* She calls herself a prophetess. Did you catch that? She was a false prophetess who worshipped the false god Baal. She seduced - them, like a tramp. The word fornication is the Greek word porneuo from where we get the English word, porno or pornography.

Pornography is lust viewed through the eyes. This sounds eerily like the episode in the garden. The lust of the eyes. Pornography, lust, and sex, through the internet, movies, music, and sin can unwillingly invite incubus and succubus into your bedroom. These practices must be abolished and renounced immediately for liberty and freedom through the blood and name of Jesus.

This has everything to do with sex, which is witchcraft practiced by incubus, that began in the Garden of Eden. Jezebel is the spirit of control which seeks to kill the prophetic voice. Do you find it strange, that Jezebel used castrated eunuchs as her employees and servants? This is what I believe happened to that Old Nacash in the Garden, a castration?

Jezebel's spirit and her witchcraft must be confronted and destroyed by the children of God, especially His prophets. His prophets should not fear retaliation as Elijah did when he wanted to die because Jezebel's vowed threats to kill him in 1 Kings 19:1-4). We know that she practiced witchcraft according to 2 Kings 9:22, *"... When Joram saw Jehu, he said, Is it peace, Jehu? And he answered, what peace, so long as the harlotries of thy mother, Jezebel, and her witchcrafts are so many?"*

Jezebel was the wife of, King Ahab, but she was a witch, and her spirit of witchcraft is steel in operation today in the church, the cities, the country, and the world. O Yes! Witches, witchcraft, and spells began in the Garden. It is in existence today, especially in the city of Angels; Los Angeles.

13.

Los Angeles: Who has Bewitched you?

When people think of witches, most of the time they think of the Wizard of Oz and the concept of a *good* witch and a bad witch. This is not true to real life because there is no such thing as a good witch. Whether it is the open evil of black magic or the hidden practices of white magic, it's still evil and an abomination unto God. No! witches do not ride on brooms, or do they?

In medieval times witches were considered to have sold their soul to Satan in exchange for magical powers and abilities. Witches are sensuous and sexual. That's why most medieval illustrations depict the witch as naked and flying through the air on a broom handle or broomstick. I find it humorous and even bemusing that after Elijah was threatened by that so-called prophetess, that witch Jezebel, he ended up under a juniper tree. The word juniper means, "broom." Coincidence? I doubt it.

The definition of a witch is basically a woman who claims to have supernatural power by a compact with the devil or evil spirits. Another name is sorceress., or high priestess. Male witches are referred to as wizards or warlocks. Witchcraft was forbidden in Israel *(Deuteronomy 18:9-14)*.

Witchcraft is divination, a divine sentence, oracle, magic, psychic ability, the practicing of fortune-telling, astrology, magical potions, and the casting of spells. Witchcraft was condemned, by all the prophets down to Micah. God spoke to him and said, *"I will cut off witchcrafts... Thou shalt have no more soothsayers (fortune tellers)."* Nacash used witchcraft in the Garden of Eden.

This craft practiced by witches is in direct contrast with the ministry of the prophets of God and designed to try to hinder or stop it. Witches operate through and utilize familiar spirits, like the way God's children work with Angels. Witchcraft, was practiced by Manasseh in *(2 Chronicles 33),* and abolished or put away during the reign of Josiah *(2 Kings 23:24)*. There were evil and good kings in Judah and Jerusalem.

"Manasseh was twelve years old when he began to reign, and he reigned fifty and five years in Jerusalem. But did that which was evil in the sight of the Lord, like unto the abominations of the heathen, whom the Lord had cast out before the children of Israel." (2 Chronicles 33: 1-2). *"And he caused his children to pass through fire in the valley of the son of Hinnom: Also, he observed times, and used enchantments, and used witchcraft, and dealt with a familiar spirit, and with wizards: he wrought much evil in the sight of the Lord, to provoke Him to anger,"* according to 2 Chronicles 33:6. Josiah took Manasseh's place as King of Jerusalem.

Josiah was eight years old when he began to reign, and he reigned in Jerusalem one and thirty years. (2 Kings 23:24). *"But in the eighteenth year of King Josiah, wherein this*

Passover was holden to the Lord in Jerusalem. Moreover, the workers with familiar spirits, and the wizards, and the images, and the idols, and the abominations that were spied in the land of Judah and in Jerusalem, did Josiah put away, that he might perform the words of the law which were written in the book that Hilkiah the priest found in the house of the Lord." 2 KINGS 23:23-24. No other king before or after Josiah obeyed the Lord and His law so completely. Witches were also known to practice necromancy.

Necromancy is the art that professes to conjure up the spirits of the dead and commune with them to predict the future, which is forbidden in the Bible. Necromancy involves demons and opens the one who practices it to demonic attack. It is actually familiar spirits impersonating the dead. Satan and his demons seek to kill, steal, and destroy, not to impart truth or wisdom. Witches are under the control of demons as well as the illuminati.

Remember I told you that the Illuminati, is in control of everything in the film, movie, radio, music, and television industry. They get many of their ideas and concepts from the Bible.

Director Steven Spielberg has admitted to this on several occasions while developing characters and concepts for some of his movies. This couldn't be more factual than in the case of the television show, *"Bewitched."* Keep in mind the definition of the word bewitched, fascinated by false representation, to affirm, profess, to speak or say. We'll come back to this part later. I will only address what it means to cast a spell, curse, and bewitch someone, something, or someplace.

The 1970's TV show, *"Bewitched," according to Wikipedia, "Samantha falls in love with New York ad executive, Darrin Stephens, and seems to be the luckiest gal alive when she marries him in the first episode of the sitcom. Then he finds out that Sam (Samantha) is one of a secret society of powerful witches and warlocks and with a twitch of her nose brings magic results. Thoroughly befuddled, Darrin makes her promise never to use her powers. She agrees and tries to settle into being the perfect suburban house wife. Her mother, Endora; however, has a different agenda. She hates that Sam has married a mortal and continually tries to break them up. Sam's other spellbinding friends pop in and out of the Stephens household as Sam tries (and fails most of the time) to live without magic."*

Now since this book is about unveiling secrets, look at what the Holy Spirit revealed. The mother-in-law's name is *Endora,* which means an eye, fountain, age, or generation. It is referring to the All-seeing eye or the third eye we talked about earlier in the book, and how it bewitches a generation.

Endora is a witch, not only on the show but I believe that could have been the witch's name in Endor, even though we aren't specifically told that.in the Bible. On top of that, her daughter, who was also a witch, was named Samantha or Sam, which is the female version of Samuel. Samuel is the prophet that the witch of Endor brought up from the dead in the Bible. The Illuminati and directors and writers of this show knew this when developing and airing this show to influence an affect an era, age, and a generation. Almost everyone watched this show when I was younger.

If you don't believe me, just watch. *1 Samuel 28:3-14, reveals, "Now Samuel was dead.... And Saul put away those that had familiar spirits (mumble, necromancer, ghost, dead spirits), and the wizards out of the land....6. And when Saul inquired of the Lord, the Lord answered him not, neither by dreams, nor by urim, nor by prophets* (you see, witches want to take the place of the Lord and His prophets)..7. *Then Saul said.... Seek me a woman that hath a familiar spirit (a witch), that I may go to her, and inquire of her* (just like when Christians go to psychics, horoscopes, and fortune tellers, and false prophets). *And his servants said to him, behold there is a woman that hath a familiar spirit at <u>Endor</u>...8...and they came to the woman by <u>night</u>* (witches like to operate in the night time, darkness)...*11.... And he said bring up Samuel..12.. And when the woman saw Samuel, she cried with a loud voice: ... 13.. And the woman said to Saul, I saw God descending up out of the earth (portal)."* It was actually Sam or Samuel, that is why she was afraid. This time it was not a familiar spirit.

Do you find it puzzling how the Illuminati was able to make this television show so accurate, thus able to release a spirit and a spell among all those who watched it? After all, it is their job to influence us by using what we hear and view. Could it be any more precise even down to the names and their meanings? The Illuminati is in control of Hollywood where all movies and television shows originate and are filmed.

The word *"Hollywood,"* has an interesting definition. The word holly is a tree, of which the wood is sought after for making magic wands as they cast spells. It is a magic wand used to cast spells. Hollywood is controlled by the lluminati, that is full of witches. Satanists are controlled by devils to cast spells on people and put them in a trance while they place curses on them.

In the book entitled, *"An Empire of Their Own: How the Jews invented Hollywood,"* by a Jewish man Neal Gabler The Nacash's plan is laid out. On page 432, Neal states, *"But what the Hollywood Jews left behind is something powerful and mysterious. What remains is a spell. A landscape of the mind the constellation of values, and attitudes and images. A history and a mythology that is part of our culture and our consciousness. What remains is the America of our imaginations and theirs."* This means that television shows like Bewitched were created to deliberately cast a spell on its viewers through its crystal ball (the Television).

Would it be even more fascinating for you to know about the original Bewitched theme song? We remember it as a tune without words, but here's another secret, the original Bewitched theme song sung by Steve Lawrence had lyrics. Just because they removed the lyrics, does not denounce or render void the intent and composition of the song to cast the spell on its listeners and viewers, to inflict witchcraft unknowingly, secretly, upon them and their lives. Here are the lyrics to *Bewitched* theme song:

Bewitched, bewitched, you've got me in your spell.
Bewitched, bewitched, you know your craft so well.
Before I knew what you were doing
I looked in your eyes.
That brand of woo you've been brewing
took me by Surprise.

You witch, you witch, One thing is for sure
That stuff, you pitch just hasn't got a cure.
My heart was under lock and key,
but somehow it got unhitched.

I never thought that I could be had
But now I'm caught and I'm kinda glad
that you, you do, that crazy voodoo
and I'm bewitched by you.
(Bewitched Theme Song)

Wow! Talk about casting a spell on an unwitty audience. The Bible says we are snared by the words of our mouth. There is a reason that the Almighty God warns us against witches and witchcraft. It is He, who can ultimately release blessings and curses. We can also do it with our own confessions, the things we say and profess, originating from that which we hear and see. The theme recording was on Columbia records. Why is this important?

According to a former witch, Satanist, freemason, and Illuminati member turned Christian, witches and demonic forces are in control with hidden occult practices (witchcraft) of Zodiac productions, which was in control of such entities as Columbia Records, RCA, and sadly Motown Records. Therefore, this theme song is no surprise.

According to John Todd's Wikipedia page he claims, *"the existence of a vast Satanic conspiracy led by an order of which is called the illuminati, including a number of Christian organizations and well-known Christian figures."*

Okay, back to the theme song and the curse. It is astounding that nine of the 17 main cast members from the TV show Bewitched died of cancer (remember in the song, *"That stuff you pitch hasn't got a cure."*).

They say cancer has no natural cure. Elizabeth Montgomery, the actress who portrayed the witch, Samantha, and proponent of gay rights and abortion, was the first to die in 1995 from colon cancer. She was the first among the rapid spread of cancer for some remaining members cast and crew. Then another seven of the main cast members, out of the 17, died of heart attacks or heart problems (in the song, *"that brand of woo you been doing took me by surprise"*). Heart attacks catch people by surprise. To top it all off, Agnes Morehead, the actress who portrayed the Mother-in-law, Endora, a professed lesbian, died from uterine cancer made a chilling statement before her death. She has been quoted as saying, *"Everyone in that picture has gotten cancer and died."* One of her last words reportedly: *"I should have never taken that part."* From this we can see that *spells* are real.

A *spell* is a form of words used as a magical charm or incantation, a state of enchantment caused by a spoken, magic spell, with the ability to control or influence people as though one hand magical power over them. A curse, or spell can also mean, writing or naming letters that form a word in correct sequence. So that means by taking out a letter or adding a letter can change the meaning of a word and change a curse to a blessing.

An example is in the very word, *"curse."* When if you spell it differently by removing the letter *"s,"* you are left with the word, *"cure."* This changes a curse into a blessing. We are to go and preach the *gospel.* Go-SPEL. We are to go and spell what God's purpose is, not the devil's or the world's. an operation of that Old Nacash in the Garden and a method that witches still use to this day. Today it is called Wicca. This is how a spell was cast over Los Angeles.

Los Angeles is better known as the City of Angels. It is a city known for spiritual activity between both holy angels and fallen angels.

In the year 1906, the Holy Spirit used a Black man who was a son of former slaves by the name of William Seymour, to release a revival spirit of God in and over the city of Los Angeles, later spread to the country and the rest of the whole world. It is the most historic revival in the history of revivals in, my opinion. The presence and power of the Holy Ghost could be felt in the atmosphere miles and miles away from the Azusa Street building when the meetings and revival took place.

On top of that, the city of Los Angeles saw many miracles. Many revivalists came to Los Angeles and flooded the city with the presence of God and His holy angels. Men like, Smith Wigglesworth, Jack Coe, A.A. Allen, William Branham, and even women like Aimee Semple McPherson, Maria Woodworth-Etter, and Kathryn Kuhlmann came to Los Angeles. They all brought revival to the city of Los Angeles in the early 1900s, but it all began at Azusa Street in Los Angeles. But what else began in Los Angeles almost six decades later?

Something happened in 1969 that closed the heavens for revival in Los Angeles and released a spirit that is still active today.

"LA's elected officials legal with kings, queens, powerful hands of state from all other countries and around the world and of course even the Pope.... The designation of official witch of Los Angeles was given by County Supervisors through a certificate. This took place in 1969 at the Hollywood bowl, in Hollywood, California. The Los Angeles County Department of Parks and Recreation in association with the Hollywood Bowl Association, sent out a press release stating that Louise Huebner the appointed and only official witch for Los Angeles County, along with a coven of witches, will involve everyone attending the concert in the casting of a spell.

This is the first time in the history of witchcraft that a spell of so great a magnitude will be cast involving so great a general public. The purpose of this gathering is to unite spiritual energies – forcefully; to alter a moment in time and to thereby create a vibration in this environment throughout all of Los Angeles County. And to cast a spell into the world and to ensure the increased sexual vitality of the County of Los Angeles.

It is important to note, that this witch had the support and participation of the, L.A. Dept. of Parks and Rec., KLAC radio, with an intro of, *"Old Black Magic,"* LADWP, Coca Cola gave cokes, Disney brought balloons, Chairman of the Board of County Supervisors, Volkswagen, Assemblymen, Assemblywomen, KTTV, Lawry's, Van de Kamp's Bakery, provided a big birthday cake, L.A. Zoo, all 78 cities of Los Angeles County at that time attended and participated}. *This was a spell cast wrapped in the guise of the party or a festival. Just one week before the spell cast at a party at the Hollywood Bowl, she was designated the official witch of L.A. This was the first, last, and only time that this has ever happened. The title was a legal document, a certificate, a scroll which was awarded to her with a title that clearly states that she was designated because of her supernatural powers. On the day of the event 11,000 people came to the Bowl for the spell casting. At the time of the spell casting, everyone chanted: "Light the flame, Bright the Fire, Red is the color of Desire." Radio, News, and television media covered this event." – Louise Huebner, L.A. Witches Story*

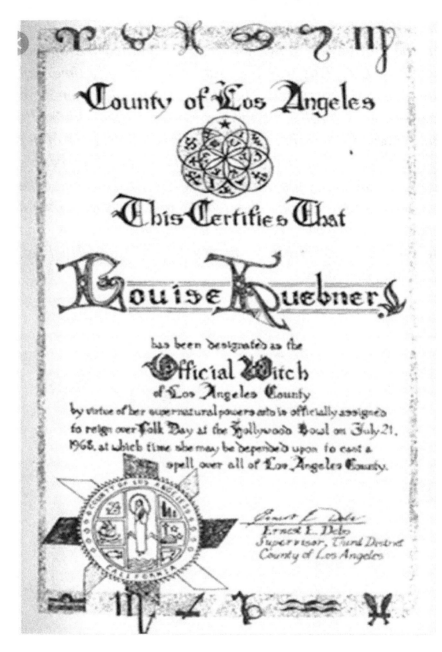

The above photo is a picture of the official document presented to Louise Huebner. This love or sex spell has not been dealt with since it has been Administered, but it is real. How else can you explain the explosion of witchcraft, witches, covens, the LGBT, gay marriage, sexual activities, molestations, rape, pedophilia, bestiality, gangs, 1992 Riots, abortion, drug use, and especially the love of money, which is the root of ALL evil. It's been a love of the things of Satan and a spirit of hate has been released through the spell.

Curses have been dispensed through this spell. I mean look at how many people were involved. This is a major stronghold! God is ready to pour out His Spirit on all flesh beginning in Los Angeles. And His love is unfeigned *(2 Corinthians 6:6)*.

God is love, and He longs to show lovingkindness to His children. In *Psalm 63:3,* it says, "...His lovingkindness is better than life." The Holy Spirit is ready to bring a revival to Los Angeles that can and will spread throughout the world. Do you know how many preachers there are in Los Angeles City alone? Hundreds. That means that there is the same amount of churches. There are close to over 2,000 churches in Los Angeles County alone. Do you know how many witches', *covens (a group of 6 male and 6 female witches, with a high priest or priestess meeting on the Sabbath)* are in Los Angeles County? Several dozens.

If the Preachers of all denominations and their congregations would come together in one gathering on one accord, and lay their *P.E.T.'s (Pride, Ego and Tradition)* down, the spell can be broken, and God's liquid love can be released through prayer and repentance. These Preachers cannot be associated or affiliated with, nor be a member of, tied to, or be benefiting from or with Freemasonry, and/ or the Illuminati, for the spell and the curse to be broken, and the tangible glory of God that was present during the

Azusa Street Revival to return in an even greater capacity, and in a new way.

It is painfully obvious that we are living in the last days. As we take our cities back, according to Joel 2:28-32, and Acts 2:1, 16-21, *"And when the day of Pentecost was fully come, they were all with one accord in one place..." 16. "But this is that which was spoken by the prophet Joel: 17. And it shall come to pass in the last days, saith God, I will pour (gush, spill) out my Spirit upon all flesh: and your sons and your daughter shall prophesy, and your young men shall see visions, and your old men shall dream dreams: 18. And on My servants and on My handmaidens I will pour out in those days of My Spirit; and they shall prophesy:" 19. And I will shew wonders in heaven above, and signs in the earth beneath; blood, and fire, and vapour of smoke: 20. The sun shall be turned into darkness, and the moon into blood, before that great and notable day of the Lord come: 21. And it shall come to pass, that whosoever shall call on the name of the Lord shall be saved."* This sounds like "revival" to me.

If we ask, God will give us the heathen (cities, nations, people) for our inheritance or possession and the uttermost parts of the earth for our possession (to seize, come upon) according to Psalms 2:8.

Los Angeles is one of the uttermost parts of the earth. It is the largest County in America, with 88 cities. It is time for another great revival. Time to move from long delays, and long waits, and impossibilities, to suddenness, possibilities, signs, wonders, miracles, and healings. What has happened in your city or nation that has opened the door to the devil and his angels, and closed the door to God and His angels?

14.

The Secret Places of The Stairs

In *Song of Solomon 2:14*, Solomon mentions, *"the Secret place of the Stairs."* It refers to a hidden portal, a staircase. Jacob saw a ladder or staircase that reached from earth to heaven and he saw angels going up and down on it. By the way, that staircase is shaped just like a DNA strand. That means that angels and demons can directly affect our DNA.

A portal is an opening, a gateway, passageway, or point of entry for the supernatural and supernatural beings. God has hidden portals all around the world, in cities, nations, regions, geographical locations, territories of land and memorials. A portal or a window, door, or gate, can also be a person.

To be a Godly portal, we need to make Jesus our Lord and Savior and get baptized and filled with the Holy Spirit with the evidence of speaking in tongues, and prophesying. Then we have the right as a Godly portal, to determine what we allow into our life, be it good or bad. Our ears and eyes act as portals in our lives.

Our Father has *given us the power to tread on serpents and scorpions, and over all the power of the enemy: and nothing shall by any means hurt us* according to Luke

10:19. Our job is to make Godly choices with the people we associate with, places we go, and what we do with our money. If we give our attention, heart, time, and money, He will give back to us, good measure pressed down shaken together and running over will men give unto us.

He also said to the Priests, *"Bring ye all the tithes into the storehouse, (wherever you are being fed) that there may be meat in mine house, and prove me now herewith, said the Lord of hosts, if I will not open the <u>windows</u> of Heaven, and pour you out a blessing, that there shall not be room enough to receive it. And I will rebuke the devourer for your sakes, and he shall not destroy the fruits of your ground; neither shall your vine cast her fruit before the time in the field, saith the Lord of hosts.* And all nations shall call you blessed: for ye shall be a delightsome land, said the Lord of hosts." Malachi 3: 10-12.

We must keep ourselves, our body, and windows Holy. But keep in mind we are to give as The Lord wills, not out of bondage or need. The new testament refers to it as offerings. The Pastor should not be trying to make you feel guilty or force you to give a certain amount of money.

According to Paul, *"Every man according as he purposeth in his heart, so let him give; not grudgingly, or of necessity: for God loveth a cheerful giver."* Paul wrote that to the Corinthian Church in 2 Corinthians 9:3. But it applies to us today.

The windows represent a timeframe and things that lurk ready to ambush us as we lie in wait. These can be blessings or curses *(Genesis 7:11, 12, Malachi 3:10)*. Moses tells us in Deuteronomy that blessings can literally *"<u>overtake us</u>."* The doors are an opening or entranceway, to unstop, a portal.

A doorway literally means a portal in the Greek. Doors provide provision and opportunities *(Psalm 24:7, Psalm 78:23-28).* In *Revelation 4:1,* John says, *"After this I looked, and behold a door was opened in Heaven...."* Doors can be opened or closed, depending on what is happening in our life.

The definition of gates is a portal, a folding entrance, an opening, city, or a split opening. The gates are for coming in and going out. Heaven, hell, cites, regions and nations all have gates *(Genesis 19:1, Psalm 24:7-9, Revelation 21:12)*

Portals begin in the third heaven (God's throne), and travel down through the second Heaven (outer space), then open on earth, in through the first Heaven (the sky and its atmosphere), and some even below the Earth.

Portals operate by opening and closing, dictated by certain activities. Signs, wonders, miracles, and healings accompany open portals to Heaven. Unanswered prayers, curses, sin, sickness, poverty, and death accompany closed portals to Heaven. In Genesis 1:14, The Lord reveals and explains what portals are for. This verse has been paraphrased by The Holy Spirit. *"And God said, Let there be brightness and favorable circumstances in the firmament of Heaven. To separate and distinguish the good from the evil; and let them be for miracles and for appointed times and seasons, daily to alter and change.*

Enoch and Elijah were taken through Portals. Nimrod built the Tower of Babel as a portal so that he could reach Heaven, to keep his kingdom of Babylon from being scattered. When people are on ONE accord, portals can be opened to reach Heaven.

The enemy can block access to the third Heaven and keep it clogged withdebris (sin), much like a kitchen sink. In *Deuteronomy 28:23*, it states, *"And thy Heaven that is over thy head shall be brass, and the earth that is under theeshall be iron."*

Isaac had to reopen and unstop portals that the enemy had closed. We are told about Isaac in Genesis 26:15,18, 15. *"For all the <u>wells</u> (to dig, declare) which his Father's servants had <u>digged</u> (seek, search out) in the days of Abraham his Father, the Philistines had <u>stopped</u> (shut, closed up, kept secret) them and filled them with earth (rubbish). Verse 18, records, "For Isaac digged again the wells of water which they had digged in the days of Abraham; For the <u>Philistines</u> (wallow self) had stopped them after the death of Abraham."* This was a familiar practice in Israel in the Old Testament. One King would tear down the high places of Baal and other false gods, and another King of Israel would put them right back up.

We read in, 2 Kings 12:3, *"But the high places were not taken away: the people sacrificed and burnt incense in the high places."* In Ephesians 6:12, we are told that spiritual wickedness likes to reside in high places. High places are where they erected altars. Altars open gates. They are erected at gates, doors and points of entry. Worshipping the true and MOST HIGH GOD at altars can open portals. How do you change an environment by opening a portal? Repentance. Repentance cancels leagues, pacts, and deals made with devils. What we must learn from the numerous instances in the Bible where high places are mentioned, whoever controls the high places controls the Heavens above it.

Whoever controls the heavens, controls the earth. Angels, deities, porters, princes, supervisors, gatekeepers, and even the Lord Himself stand on top of the portal. This is confirmed in Genesis 28:12,13, *"12. And he dreamed, and behold a ladder set up on the earth, and the top of it reached to heaven: and behold the angels of God ascending and descending on it. 13. And, behold, the Lord stood above it....."* The Lord stood above what? The ladder or the portal? God's portals are for the traffic of Angels and for the presence of God, for the glory and power of the eternal and the miraculous realm to invade time.

"Demonic inspired altars offer worship to appease, empower, and release the influence of Satan and his fallen angelic host from the second Heaven. God inspired altars offer worship to extol honor and release the influence of God and His Holy Angelic host from the third Heaven."
– Portals p.37 – Dr. Patti Amsden

Another reliable source on portals is John Paul Jackson. He was an American author, teacher, conference speaker, and founder of Streams Ministries International. He focused on supernatural topics like dreams, visions, and dream interpretations as found in the Bible according to Wikipedia. He was also a man that I learned a great deal from about dreams and visions.

In John Paul Jackson's book, *Heavenly Portals,* *"A heavenly portal is a spherical opening of light that offers divine protection by which angels and heavenly beings can come and go, without demonic interference. God had designed portals to begin in the third Heaven, travel through the second Heaven, and open upon Earth."* Furthermore, John Paul Jackson agrees that Jerusalem is a portal, and the center of the Earth. It is a major portal on the face of the Earth. It is the main current event in the world in December of 2017.

On December 7, 2017, U.S.A. President, Donald Trump, has recognized Jerusalem as Israel's capital, and to move the US Embassy from Tel Aviv to Jerusalem. President Trump's Jerusalem decision has drawn mixed reactions around the World.

The United Nations General Assembly members voted to overwhelmingly condemn the U.S. decision on Jerusalem. They voted to reject Trump's recognition of Jerusalem as Israel's capital. Protest have escalated and hostile demonstrations are a result of the inflamed tensions around the world.

Since God is using President Trump, maybe that is the reason that the Los Angeles Times printed an article entitled, *"I Put a Spell on you Mr. President."* Thousands of witches, and believers (like witches) and all others over the world performed, *"A spell to bind Donald Trump and all those who abet him, under the waning crescent moon."* I can't remember witches coming against Obama. Can you? Probably, because they didn't. But since President Trump is fulfilling God's plan, the Nacash plans to retaliate.

On December 22,2017 in San Francisco, California, an Isis supporter, an ex-Marine, was arrested for plotting a Christmas bombing of San Francisco on Fisherman's Wharf on Pier 39. God is pleased with Trump's decision about Jerusalem. President Trump is the first American president to take the step to make Jerusalem the capital of Israel, since the founding of Israel in 1948. Also see 1 Kings 15:4, 11 Kings 19:34, 11 Chronicles 6:6 and 12:13.

Jerusalem became the capital of the Kingdom of Israel under King David in 1000 BCE. Solomon built the first

Holy Temple about 40 years later. Also, Goliath's head that David cut off is buried in Jerusalem.

In 1 Samuel 17:54, David slew *Goliath, "And David took the head of the Philistine, and brought it to Jerusalem; but he put his armour in his tent."* Goliath's head was buried at Calvary, Golgotha, or Place of the Skull.

In the _Weekly World News_, on May 25, 1993, Dr. Martin, a German archaeologist, discovered Goliath's skull with a stone still embedded in its head. That is probably why Golgotha is called, *"The Place of the Skull."*

This was done to fulfill the prophecy of Genesis 3:15, *"And I will put enmity between thee and the woman, and between thy seed and her seed; it shall bruise thy head, and thou shall bruise his heel."* David crushed the head of Satan when he killed Goliath, an enemy of God's children. Jesus' heel was bruised when nails where driven through them on Calvary's Cross.

Within the last 8 years, there has been a flurry of terror attacks here in America. One of the biggest ones killing 49 at the Orlando night club in June. But as I was writing this book, on February 14, 2018 a mass shooting was committed at Majory Stoneman Douglas High School in Parkland, Florida. Nikolas Cruz was arrested, and seventeen people were killed and 17 more were injured.

The largest to date was the Las Vegas shooting that occurred on the night of Sunday, October 1, when a or some shooters opened fire on a crowd of unsuspecting concertgoers at the Route 91 Harvest, music festival on the Las Vegas Strip in Nevada, leaving 58 people dead and 851 injured. The worst, of course was over 3,000 that died on September 1, 2001.

I believe that because of what President Trump did, by

agreeing with David and the Bible and making Jerusalem the capital of Israel, God has opened a special portal to put a hedge of divine protection around the United States of America, to make America not just Great again, but Safe again as well.

Besides, Jesus was crucified in Jerusalem. His blood was shed for all Mankind; for our salvation, deliverance, healing, and for all our needs to be met. The open portal over the U.S.A, will allow Jesus to be Lord over the USA. and the communication from the second to cease and communication from third Heaven to flourish.

We know that there is a second Heaven because there is a third Heaven. We can't have a third floor in a house without a second floor. Also, in the book of Daniel chapter 10 we are told of the story of how the Lord sent an answer to Daniel's prayers through an angel. It took him 21 days *(the exact amount of time that Daniel went on a fast to receive the answer to his prayer)* to reach his destination, which was Daniel, because of the spiritual warfare and fight in battle that he had to withstand from a spirit (Prince of Persia) and wickedness in high places from a fallen angel of equal rank. The angel had to call for the assistance from the Angel Michael, one of the chief princes who outranked the Spirit being to help him win that fight. This is the reality of the spiritual warfare that we are engaged in on a daily.

Tom Horn explains to us in, <u>Nephilim Stargates</u> on page 98, *"In Persian theology, this upholding spirit would have been identified as Ahriman - enemy of Ahura-Mazda. According to Persian religion, Ahriman was the death dealer.*

The powerful and self-existing evil spirit, from whom war and all other evils had their origin. He was the chief of the Cacodaemons, or fallen angels, expelled from heaven for their sins. After their expulsion, the Cacodaemons took up their abode in the space between heaven and earth and, there, established their domain... From the sky above, the Cacodaemons could intrude upon and attempt to corrupt humans below."

High places are basically elevated platforms. You know like the Hollywood sign or even think about Jacob's ladder, or the gods upon the mount of Olympus, Moses on top of Mount Sinai, Elijah on top of Mount Carmel, Watchers descending on Mount Hermon. Or the best one; the defeat by the returning Christ Jesus upon the Mount of Olives. Most signs are placed in high places to announce whose territory it is. When there is a sign over a door it declares where you are going when you walk through it. And despite the omnipotence, omniscience, omnipresence, and eternal immutability, of El Elyon, The Most High God, whoever sacrifices at the altar, the high place and is more fully submitted to their god, possesses the territory, and the victory.

There are some astounding results that can occur when a portal is opened. Especially a portal opened to the second heaven and the fallen Angels. In another excerpt from Tom Horn, Nephilim Stargates, p. 21,22, it states, *"in 1918, famed occultist Aleister Crowley attempted to create a dimensional vortex that would bridge the gap between the world of the seen and the unseen . The ritual (sex, Omophagia- eating raw flesh), called the Alamantrah working... ...became successful when a presence manifested itself through a rift.*

He called the being lam and drew a portrait of it... ...30 years later cofounder of the jet propulsion laboratory

Jack Parsons and his pal L. Ron Hubbard (Church of Scientology founder), conducted a 2nd ritual (a sex ritual) called the Babylon working, in an attempt to reopen the gateway opened by Crowley... .... instead they wanted the whore of Babylon and they believe they succeeded and she walks the earth today." -   Nephilim Stargates p.21,22

As you can see supernatural forces and beings can be unleashed when a person conducts a ritual in order to open a portal. Witches are secretly notorious for hiding things in high places in order to stake a claim on the territory. It's usually a mountain or a hill. Witches and occultists place pyramids, upside down crosses, symbols resembling male and female genitals, cursing rods, and all kinds of cursing issues. They strategically select areas (high places) where portals are already established through major events. They sacrifice by praying, chanting, fasting, doing enchantments, and spells, and laying curses. They even commit human sacrifice and blood drinking.

Witches chant, fast, and pray for the demise of God's children in order to bring diseases and sickness upon them. And because of this many of God's children are defeated. But how can this happen? Satan is not more powerful than God, and he never will be. How can Godly people suffer defeat at the hands of Satan?   Well, there is a perplexing story in the Bible. It is a quandary when you consider and ponder it.

In 2 Kings chapter 3, Israel is winning this war against the Moabites, and two kings of Israel (Judah, and Jehosophat) have just joined forces. The King of Moab is really scared, because they are stripping the land bare, and fulfilling the prophecy of Elisha. Israel was on a roll and had possession of that portal until the unthinkable took place. What happened next is the exact principle that the Illuminati lives and swears by? HUMAN SACRIFICE! Human sacrifice is the act of killing humans as an offering to a deity as part of a ritual. Israel was defeated because the King of Satan (Moab) sacrificed his oldest son.

Look at what is stated in 2Kings 3:26,27: 26. *And when the king of Moab (an incestuous son Of Lot) saw that the battle was too sore for him, He took with him seven hundred men that drew swords, to break through even unto the king of Edom: but they could not. 27. Then he took his Eldest son that should have reigned in his stead And offered him for a burnt offering upon a wall. And there was great indignation against Israel: And they departed from him and returned to Their own land.*

Every time I read that I wonder how could that happen? It is surprising that the Lord God tested Abraham with a possible human sacrifice when He instructed Abraham to sacrifice his son Isaac and offer him as a burnt offering to test his submission. The lord sent an Angel to stop him right before he did it. Abraham sacrificed a ram instead, and God said to Abraham through the Angel, *"..for now I know that thou fearest God, seeing thou hast not withheld thy son..."* (Genesis 22:1-19).

It defies logic that anything can defeat the people of God. But the children of Israel were defeated. Not just in this instance but many times before. We suffer defeat that's just as perplexing.

We must understand that which is sent by the enemy to erode our faith and occupy the territory. It was not a whimsical decision for the king to sacrifice his oldest son, who was to reign as king after he passed. It was agony and excruciatingly painful for him to do that. Who inspired or caused that decision? Satan. He called his god Baal, Baal is a devil. Whoever is more submitted to their god when it comes to battle for territory wins the war. Nothing is mightier or stronger than God. But if witches, and charmers are more submitted to their god and willing to do and sacrifice whatever is necessary required by it; they win. The Illuminati has and will sacrifice celebrities and camouflage their cause of death, to stay undetected.

Sacrifice couldn't be more evident than in the case of Los Angeles, Hollywood, and the world. The Illuminati spread witchcraft through blood sacrifice when John F. Kennedy was inaugurated as 35th president of the United States of America. It is well known that President Kennedy made a speech which was against and aimed to expose *"secret"* societies. Frank Sinatra sang a rendition of the song, *"That Old Black Magic,"* at the inauguration ceremony. He changed words in the song from black magic to Jack magic. This is enchantment, and witchcraft. And it is the same tactic that the Old Nacash used in the Garden of Eden.

Kennedy whose name means *"helmeted chief,"* was a world renown figure, and to cast a spell on the world you need a world renown sacrifice. John F. Kennedy was assassinated November 22, 1963 at 12:30 pm in Dallas, Texas, while riding in a presidential motorcade in Dealey plaza. An occult, ritual, human sacrifice! And, of course Louise Huebner predicted his death, and *(incidentally opened her weekly radio show with the song That Old Black Magic)* pure witchcraft, and prognostication at its best. Next Satan needed to use the Rulers of the Darkness of This world, the Illuminati to sacrifice another world renown figure. But this time one who was black and revered in America. They needed to sacrifice a King.

Martin Luther King Jr. was an avid proponent against the secret society, Freemason led, KKK. And he also distanced himself from the secret society Boule, towards the end of his life. He was an Activist, American Baptist Minister and a man of God. He became a visible spokesperson and leader in the civil rights movement from 1954 through 1968. He fought for equal rights, and liberty, and justice for all. Martin Luther king was assassinated, April 4, 1968 at the Lorraine Hotel in Memphis Tennessee. Satan now had another notable sacrifice of a king to inflame the ills of racism even further and set the tone for the future of America.

Dr. King was set up and the CIA (Freemason, secret society) and the govt, was found guilty in a court of law for conspiracy to kill Dr. King. In 1999, Dr. Martin Luther King's family won a civil lawsuit proving the U.S. government was responsible for his assassination. The same CIA rumored to have killed President Kennedy (Incidentally, there are eerie, astounding similarities between the lives, presidency, and assassinations of Abraham Lincoln and John F. Kennedy). You see, all of these secret societies are run by the Nacash and his angels and work together as a unified network to execute a plot. This human sacrifice of Dr. king took place during Passover season and in the same year that the spell cast would be performed,1968. Witches understand portals are opened during festivals or feast times, like Feast of Passover, Feast of Tabernacles, and Feast of Pentecost.

The cover of Time Magazine in January 2018 is entitled, *"1968: The year that shaped a generation."* This is a very significant year, because the last of the major human sacrifices to enslave the people of this world was to execute one in the very city that the spell would be released, Los Angeles.

Robert F. Kennedy the Presidential candidate and brother of President John F. Kennedy was assassinated at the Ambassador Hotel in Los Angeles on June 5, 1968, shortly after winning the California presidential primaries in the 1968 election. This would be just a month before The Official Witch of Los Angeles would perform the largest spell cast the world has ever seen even to this very day. But a blood sacrifice was necessary in the same city.

The Illuminati is well aware of this necessity for power and authority over a region. But why three sacrifices? People say that celebrity deaths always come in threes. The number three represents conformity.

Louise Huebner sacrificed to a three - headed goddess named Hekate, requiring three notable, high ranking blood sacrifices. During the Spell cast at the Hollywood Bowl, the witch gave every one (including children) two red candles, salt, chalk and garlic. They were instructed to use the chalk to draw a circle around themselves and then sprinkle salt inside the circle (hexagram). Then they were told to light the two red candles. But not before placing a clove of garlic at the head of the circle. The garlic was to appease the goddess Hekate, the deity to whom she was worshipping, offering sacrifices, and ushering into the sex atmosphere over and in the city.

Hekate (hundred) is the three - headed goddess of magic, witchcraft, the night, moon, doorways, creatures of the night, ghosts and necromancy, and is depicted with two flaming torches. She resembles the Statue of liberty a little bit. She was supposedly capable of good and evil. This is similar to good and bad witches. But all witches are evil. Hekate is also associated with light, entranceways, knowledge of herbs and poisonous plants. She is the Mother of Angels and the Cosmic World. She relates to borders, city walls, doorways, crossroads, thresholds, gates, and boundaries with realms outside or beyond the world of the living. Hekate is the spirit over portals. Therefore, it is no wonder that the people at the Hollywood Bowl were duped, lured, and seduced into chanting a spell and releasing the spirit of Hekate over the city of Los Angeles, America, the world, and the entire cosmos. The candles represented the torches that Hekate held in her hands.

Since they were all together in one accord, the spell cast was successful, and the city now belonged to Satan, legally! This portal was now clogged and stopped up and fallen angels and deities were able to perpetrate and masquerade in disguise as angels of the Lord. Just like in the Garden of Eden.

However, these are fallen angels who are occupying thrones in Los Angeles, and all over the world. Instead of receiving from Jesus Christ (The Anointed) from the 3rd Heaven, they receive from false Christs from the second heaven. Frauds, imposters, witches, false Christs and Anti-christs present themselves as look- a-likes and are able to deceive and push the Antichrist agenda.

15.

ANTICHRIST:
THE LOOK-A-LIKE

Many people are being deceived by antichrists, that are basically look-a-likes. Their job is to present a false reality and make one appear as another. The definition of the word antichrist is, instead of or in place of the Anointed; an opponent of the Messiah. There are some scriptures that explain and define this term. 2 John 1:7 records, *"For many deceivers (imposters, seducing, misleaders) are entered into this world, who confess not that Jesus Christ is come in the flesh. This is a deceiver and an antichrist."*

Even though everyone is aware of the Antichrist, the bible states that there are many antichrists even during biblical times, let alone today. The Apostle John confirms this in 1 John 2:18, by stating, *"Little children, it is the last time: and as ye have heard that antichrist shall come, even now there are many antichrists (plural); whereby we know that it is the last time."* To cap it off, Jesus himself warns us in Mark 13:5,6 saying, 5." *And Jesus answering them began to say, take heed lest any man deceive you: 6. For many shall come in my name, saying, I am Christ (Anointed); and shall deceive many."* He was talking to the body of Christ, but before we explore that, how is it evident in the world that we live in every day.

Deception is one of the major wiles of Satan. This is the weapon that he used in the garden of Eden and the same one being used today. It's like the veil has been pulled over our eyes to hide the truth from us. The job of the Nacash and his angels is to deceive the whole world, by any means necessary. We must remember there is enmity between the serpent seed and the seed of the woman through adoption and bloodline. That is why when you see or hear anything on the mainstream media, you must judge and evaluate it because it is probably a lie or twisted half - truth.

Since the 1950's the CIA (Central Intelligence Agency) has had their hand at controlling many top news outlets for the purpose of spreading false narratives and propaganda. This operation also consisted of bribing journalists to skew public opinion in their favor. It wasn't until 1975, that *Operation Mockingbird* became known, but only some of the public realized that they had been duped. It was a massive disinformation campaign. It is obviously still in use today as the news is still nothing but scripted news that fits their Antichrist agenda and distracts people from the truth.

Always question the news that you are given from the media. If we believe what the Illuminati tells us, we will forever be living in the land of make believe.

The land of make believe is like The Matrix where everything is the opposite of what it really is. A virtual reality. Where a woman can be a man and a man can be a woman. A world where marriage is no longer just between a man and a woman. A world where there is an outlet of social media, with Apps like Facebook, Snapchat, Instagram, and Twitter, where you can present yourself to be whatever you desire to be regardless of the truth. A world where a true man of God is imprisoned and labeled a criminal for telling the truth. And an evil heathen can present a pretty packaged lie and be lauded for it.

Speaking of packages, did you know to appease the LGBTQ community and package an acceptance gospel, there is a Queen James Bible. What a travesty! That's why you must be careful of the Bible translations that you read from. The most recently updated version of the N.I.V. incorporated some gender language changes and removes over 64,000 words. It is produced by Zondervan, who is owned by Harper Collins who publishes the *NIV, Satanic Bible,* and the *Joy of Gay Sex.* The name Jehovah does not appear in this updated version of the Bible and whole verses are gone *(Acts8:37, Matt. 7:21,18:11, 23:14, Mark 7:16, 9:44, 1:26, 15:28, Luke 17:36, 23:17, John 5:4, Acts 15:34, 24:7, 28:29, and Rom. 16:24).*

While I am writing about the subject of Bibles, and Antichrist; did you know that the DSM psychiatric bible has changed pedophilia from being a *"mental illness,"* to a *"sexual orientation."* That means that those in the psychiatric profession label pedophilia as normal sexual behavior. They MUST BE CRAZY!! In fact, how's this for a secret, Barak Obama sent a Memo to the Justice Department while he was president that listed twelve sexual perversions, that they wanted to legalize. This includes bestiality, polygamy, incest, and having sex with boys and girls. We can connect these sexual activities to Eden's Garden and the sex spell cast on Los Angeles by Louise Huebner in 1968. Pedophilia demonic spirits were released and dispensed at the Hollywood Bowl.

After the Pizza gate exposure, many people have been opened to the deep-state pedophile rings from Hollywood, to the Vatican, to the CIA, etc. Satanic networks are kidnapping, abducting, raping, ritually murdering children through human sacrifice. Many now adult Hollywood actors and actresses are now speaking out about the pedophiles. There are even pedophile priests and some Pastors. The Catholic Church confirms this by paying billions of dollars in sexual abuse lawsuit settlements and allowing the priests to continue in that occupation, and never spend time in jail and continue to molest children.

Unfortunately, when it comes to Satanic ritual abuse, many people dismiss the revelation as a *"conspiracy theory."* Despite what doubters believe, Satanist do engage in sex magic rituals, and as I have mentioned before, HUMAN SACRIFICE. Black Magic Magician Aleister Crowley taught and influenced any of his followers that they can receive power through raping and abusing children.

There are documented cases of pedophile rings from the *Franklin Cover-Up to the CIA's MKULTRA program, Operation Peter Pan, and Pizza Gate.* In fact according to many sources over 50% of U.S. Congress are members of *NAMBLA (North American Man Boy Love Association).*

In the late 1970's and early 1980's, thousands of children were abused in daycare facilities, and most victims reported occult rituals that were performed. At Presidio military daycare in California in the late 80's, children were forced to drink urine and eat feces; and their bodies were smeared with blood. At least five children were diagnosed with the sexually transmitted disease Chlamydia, and one boy tested positive for AIDS. On top of that 60 children showed signs of abuse that included vaginal discharge, sleep disturbances, nightmares, genital soreness, rashes, fear of the dark, sexually provocative language and sexually provocative behavior. Remember the Nacacsh transmitted the first STD to Eve. That's where it began in Eden's garden. Satan always comes after the children, and they must be protected.

For more details on this subject read the books, *"The Franklin Cover-Up,"* by John DeCamp, *"Pedophile and Empire...,"* by Joachim Hagopian, and *"Eaters of Children,"* by John Cirucci. I know these stories are sick but legalizing the raping of children is not that uncommon in the agenda of the Antichrist.

The epitome of an Antichrist was when on Saturday, July 25, 2015 the Satanic Temple in Detroit unveiled a 9-foot-tall bronze statue of the goat god transgender Nephilim Baphomet. It weighed almost a ton. He has hooves for feet and with his legs crossed, a pentagram and torch between his eyes, with what appears to be an erect phallus, and a girl on his left and a boy on his right; both looking at him admirably. They are currently trying to erect this Satanic look-alike around the country. Daniel saw The Baphomet years ago. It (Baphomet) or he/she is an ancient being.

"And as I was considering, behold an he goat came from the west on the face of the whole earth, and touched not the ground: and the goat had a notable horn between his eyes." – Daniel 8:5

Many find this statue noncontroversial and feel there might be some element of truth to it. However, Satan always offers something that looks like the real thing and comes across as the truth. Everything about him and his kingdom is opposite of God and is therefore false.

The word *false* is defined as deliberately made or meant to deceive, and what is not actually so. Myriads of cults were birthed from fallen angel contact. It is no wonder that this word is tossed around so flippantly and designated as a label for major catastrophes. The world calls them *"false flags."* The Bible mentions false Christs, teachers, apostles, prophets, reports, witnesses, doctrine, vision, dreams, divination, oaths, swearers, accusers, and brethren. Therefore, falsehood exists!

According to Wikipedia, *"a false flag refers to covert operations designed to deceive; the deception creates the appearance of a party (group or nation) being responsible for some activity, disguising the actual source of responsibility."*

Could wars have been deliberately started by the Illuminati through false flags and fake news? How about the Spanish American War and the bombing of the USS Maine? Then there's the bombing in Lusitania to start World War 1? Are false flags the reasons for these wars? What about Pearl Harbor in World War 2, or the Gulf of Tonkin and the Vietnam War? This couldn't be truer than in the case concerning the collapse of the Twin Towers and the terrorist attack on 9/11 to destabilize the Middle East.

Satan uses the government ran by the Illuminati to push his Antichrist agenda through fear and death. False flags are catastrophic, staged events blamed on political enemies to start war or enact laws of national security. Some have real victims, and some don't. There is a secret force behind this, and it started in the Garden.

President John F. Kennedy made some telling comments 7 days before his assassination. *"There's a plot in this country to enslave every man, woman and child.*

Before I leave this high and noble office, I intend to expose this plot. " This may have been part of that plot? Are there ways to spot false flags? The Nacash has a plot, But God has a plan.

Have you ever noticed that there is always a drill taking place at the same time as, and near the tragedy? There also seems to be some fore-knowledge or premonition of the event happening.

The Simpsons T.V. show often *"predicts"* events that occur in real life shortly thereafter. They mix in crisis actors (the same crisis actors over and over), combined with a lack of picture and video evidence, an easily contained crime scene, and the official story changing over and over. Not to mention the eye witnesses conflicting account of multiple shooters when it comes to shootings that are blamed on a lone gunman. Then the witnesses mysteriously turn up missing or dead. How is it that the patsy suspect is always so accurate without any military training? The patsy gets killed, drugged, or suicided and evidence mysteriously gets destroyed. The problem is that nearly all mass shooters in the last 20 years were on mind altering, psychiatric drugs. They were *MK Ultra* or mind-controlled victims.

The CIA created project *MK ULTRA* to control human consciousness. Wow! That sounds like the Tree of Knowledge of good and evil, and The Nacash. It's all a plot by the New World Order for gun control and the confiscation of arms. The political agenda overcomes their reactions, grief is shunned, and there is an immediate call for gun control.

In 1991 William Cooper wrote a book entitled, *"Behold A Pale Horse."* In chapter 12 *(The Secret Government)* he makes the following statement, *"The government encouraged the manufacture and importation of military firearms for the criminals to use. This is intended to foster a sense of insecurity, which would lead the American people to voluntarily disarm themselves by passing laws against firearms. Using drugs and hypnosis on mental patients in a process called Orion, the CIA inculcated the desire in these people to open fire on schoolyards and thus inflame the antigun lobby. This plan is well under way, and so far is working perfectly. The middle class is begging the government to do away with the second amendment.* " This was written in 1991 and today in 2018 that plan is in full effect.

It's a plot of deception that is supposed to be kept in secret. It is clear manipulation through witchcraft behind the scenes. How else can we explain the fact that during our drought, Californians were so desperate for water they would turn to magic, spiritualism, and witches to find it? How about turning to Jesus Christ the creator of all and pray for rain, like Elijah? But it is an Antichrist agenda, so what should we expect?

When Nestles Chairman of the Board makes statements such as, *"Human Beings don't have a right to water."* It only furthers the narrative of the serpent seed, and Cain's Illuminati blood-line are alive and in positions of power and authority. The Nacash has his Nephilim seed here on earth and they are human look-a-likes. They look like us. Since they are in charge Satan uses them to change God's plan. From lesbian and gay marriage to transgenderism, and even now today, the AFA has reported that pedophilia officially classified as a sexual orientation. AN UNBELIEVABLE ABOMINATION!

The governor of California Jerry Brown has even made it illegal to use the words husband and wife in California. This an Antichrist agenda, and against the very design of God from the very beginning.

Satan is also forcing children and adults to receive vaccine shots, and flu injections. It has been proven that these vaccine shots for babies lead to Autism and the flu shots have led to cancer and many deaths. That's what the Nacash does, he makes one thing appear beneficial, when it is detrimental. He hasn't changed from the Garden of Eden. Sadly, when Holistic doctors have disclosed the dangers of vaccines they end up mysteriously dead. Most of them have been young and in the prime of their careers. Sounds like the Nacash and The Illuminati to me.

It isn't hard to guess who is behind these deaths when laws are passed enforcing the consumption of these viruses (vaccines). The CDC *(Center for Disease Control),* based in Atlanta Georgia, recommends 69 shots by the age of 18. Vaccines have been used as population control or reduction or Agenda 21 and are a form of biological warfare. In most of these cases the vaccine is deadlier and more dangerous than the disease it prevents.

California lawmakers passed SB277 which makes vaccines mandatory by denying parents, the option to opt out under religious or personal beliefs. Under this real-life scenario, the people are victims. Unfortunately, many of the LGBTQP are also victims of the Antichrist agenda.

That Old Nacash has always successfully attempted to manipulate human DNA. But some things are just beyond diabolical. There is a chemical called *Astrazine*; a synthetic compound used as an agricultural herbicide. Monzanto has hired American biologist and professor of Integrative

Biology at University of California, Berkeley, Tyrone B. Hayes to experiment and find out if *astrazine* changes the sexual orientation of straight frogs into homosexual frogs, and it did. They then pumped this chemical into the waters of the ghettos of the USA.

Nobody is born homosexual. According to Dr. N.E. Whitehead, *"Identical twins have identical genes. If homosexuality was a biological condition produced inescapably by the genes (e.g. eye color), then if one identical twin was homosexual, in 100% of the cases his brother would be too. But we know that about only 38% of the time is the identical twin brother homosexual...this conclusion has been well known in the scientific community for a few decades but has not reached the general public. Indeed, the public increasingly believes the opposite."* How could a secret plot that originated in the Garden of Eden so long ago, work to perfection in this present day and age?

Satan has always been putting himself in the place of Christ for eons. His infiltration has been effective in the Freemason led churches. Charles Spurgeon said, *"A time will come where instead of shepherds feeding the sheep, the church will have clowns entertaining the goats."* That time is now because Satan has his ministers in positions of leadership. Members of his Covert network of the five-fold ministry of Apostles, Prophets, Teachers, Evangelists, and Pastors. The people are deceived because a lack of real discernment and are persuaded that the look-alike is genuine. If we could only see them in their true form instead of being fooled by the Nacash, we would be startled. Satan's ministers can transfigure or disguise their external condition (metashematizo). It is a grand scheme.

Satan has a plot, that God is always aware of, but he can't change God's plans.

Many witnesses have reported of celebrities, and famous people shapeshifting into a reptilian form, and quickly shapeshifting back into a regular human. Reptilian form as a serpent or snake would be? Transforming themselves just like the Bible states in second Corinthians. Ferocious wolves disguised in shepherd's clothing. Many are standing behind our pulpits. Even though we are told to watch for them, and that we would recognize them, we don't. Yet few know what to watch for and fewer know how to discern. Without being filled with The Holy Spirit it is impossible to recognize the false and discern it from the genuine. Because they are designed to be a look-alike. Just like clones.

Human Cloning is the creation of a genetically identical copy of a human. The term is used to refer to artificial human cloning, which is the reproduction of human cells and tissue. I want you to notice the words copy and artificial. A false representation. The Nacash is even using Artificial intelligence by making robots, and computers with human capabilities. Look at what this verse in Revelation states, *"And he had power to give life unto the image of the beast, that the image of the beast should both speak and cause that as many as would not WORSHIP the IMAGE of the beast should be killed. "* – Revelation 13:15

Satan is the master cloner. All he needs is DNA. He uses his seed to do what he says, and once he is done with them, he then kills (sacrifices) them and clones them and uses their body. Remember when Satan contended with Michael for the body of Moses. The Lord Himself had to rebuke him. Was Satan trying to clone Moses? There are number of underground secret cloning facilities around the world.

An underground bunker is where Area 51 is located. This is where all Alien and extraterrestrial evidence is held by the government. This leads me to the conclusion that the aliens are really Nephilim connected to Cain's lineage and a reptilian connection through the transforming serpent. To confirm this story, I must refer you to the Los Angeles Times Newspaper of January 29, 1934, by Jean Bosquet. *The article was entitled, Lizard Peoples Catacomb City Hunted. DID STARNGE PEOPLE LIVE UNDER SITE OF LOS ANGELES 5000 YEARS AGO?* This could be the land of Nod (vanishing point), where Cain went.

There is a layout of a map of an underground city with tunnels, passages and caverns, gold, rooms, and a school. They were human beings called lizard people? You must read the article! If there is no connection, then why are the cloning facilities secret, and located underground? I believe it is because the Illuminati has been fooling the masses with a look -alike. Your favorite celebrity, musician, preacher, actor, politician, or professional athlete may not even be the REAL them. It's just another artificial, false, copy of them. But it is NOT them. Just like the Antichrist is a look-alike but it's NOT JESUS! The devil deceives the whole world. That Old Nacash's job is to beguile and seduce us into accepting another Jesus, another spirit, and another gospel.

16.
Another Jesus, Another Spirit, Another Gospel

In the Garden of Eden Eve was deceived and believed the Nacash when he preached another way to get the things that she desired. Another way for Eve to be prosperous and attain what she did not have. He told her, *"Ye shall not surely die."* He preached *another Jesus* (savior) to her.

Next Eve received *another Spirit* (to chill) from the Nacash. She got chills and goose bumps. It was the spirit of lust and desire against God's specific instructions of not eating from that tree. She saw how good it could be good to be with the Nacash, and how pleasant he was to look at. She desired him. Lastly, Eve accepted *another gospel* (announce good news), because it was good news to her, to find out that she could have what was forbidden without ramifications. He told her, *"It will be the best experience that you could imagine. It will feel good. Your eyes will be opened, you'll be wise and just like the gods. You will be glowing. God won't punish you."* (Wives can glow after sex/making love with their husbands).

Oh! How wrong she was! And how wrong are many today who are receiving a watered-down grace gospel, without any consequences. This gospel does not preach against sin, repentance, holiness, or the true filling of The

Holy Spirit. They preach *another Jesus,* the people receive *another spirit,* and they accept *another gospel.* Paul tells us how this all began in the Garden of Eden in 2 Corinthians 11:3,4.

It reads, 3. *"But I fear, lest by any means, as the serpent beguiled Eve through his subtilty (clever deceit), so your minds should be corrupted (to lead away a Christian church) from the simplicity (free from pretense, and hypocrisy) that is in Christ."*

4. For if he that cometh preacheth another Jesus, (Ieosus) whom we have not preached, or if ye receive another (different) spirit , which ye have not received, or another gospel, (good tidings) which ye have not accepted, ye might bear (to hold oneself up against) well with him."

Another Jesus:

I remember recently having a conversation with someone who has was once a Christian but has abandoned the faith. She has turned towards praying to ancestors and the ways of the Hebrew Israelites. She believes the Jesus that she grew up learning about was false. He was not a white Jesus, according to her, and she has been lied to all her life in the church. She even brought to the fore-front the fact that his name is Yeshua and not Jesus.

Let's discuss the name of Jesus before I continue with this story. In the 1611 KJV the name Jesus was spelled *Iesus.* It was not spelled with the letter J. The letter I was changed into the letter J forming a new letter. Some claim the J sound did not exist before the 16th century but scholars have proven that it did.

The letter I represented three sounds. When followed by

a consonant I was pronounced "I" (Israel). When "I" was followed by a vowel it was pronounced "J" (Jezreel). The I sound when followed by a vowel can also be pronounced "Y" (Yisrael). It seems to be a matter of choice. It is not correct to claim that" J" should be pronounced "ya" or "ye."

Therefore, it is not correct to pronounce the name Jesus as Yahshua or Yeshua. In the Hebrew alphabet there is no "Y" or "W." So, it is also incorrect to pronounce the name Jehovah as Yewhew. In the Hebrew the name Jesus would be Jesous, but in English it is pronounced Jesus. In Numbers 13:16, Moses changed the name of Oshea to Jehoshua, or Joshua in English. Jesus means salvation and Joshua means deliverer. Therefore, the name "JESUS," is an original name, and it holds power! All right, now back to the woman.

I asked her what turned her away from Jesus? She said, *"I prayed for a husband and God sent him to me. We got married and then he changed, and we got divorced."* I asked her why she blamed God for that? Everyone has a free will! It was because she prayed He answered and let her down in her own words. As if the ancestors posing as familiar spirits are more reliable and faithful! I asked, *"What could Jesus to do to get you back?"* But, then it dawned on me. The real Jesus does not have to do <u>anything</u> else.

He came, lived, suffered, and died on a brutal cross for her sake. Our sake! He has risen and is alive today, reigning as The King of Kings and Lord of Lords! He is on the throne and at the right hand of the Father forever more, interceding on our behalf. He doesn't have to do anything else! Jesus has done more than enough and certainly more than any of us deserve. But she did have a point about this other Jesus.

Often, there are images of a long, blonde hair, blue-eyed effeminate androgynous, looking images of a supposed Jesus. This picture is as much of a lie of a dark-skinned Jesus with long, thick dreadlocks. Although the dominant presence of black people is evident throughout the Bible, it clearly states that Jesus was Jewish. This god, or fallen angel is Mithras, another Jesus or an ascended master. Mithras is the Roman sun god that seems to resemble Jesus and mimics the same life story.

"Scholars have noted how closely the story of the god Mithra seems to resemble the story of Jesus. "Mithras was to be king and shepherd like Christ. He was to give life and healing to the sick. He would raise the dead and loose the bonds of the captives. He was to destroy his enemies" (Religion of Babylon and Assyria pp. 71, 72)

This Mithras is another Jesus, and part of the deception that is constructed around Christmas; the supposed timed of Jesus Birth. However, Mithras was born on the 25th of December, The Natalis Invicti Solis, the birthday of the unconquered sun (Two Babylons, Alexander Hislop, p.98). It was a festival in honor of the Pagan sun god. *"Jesus Christ was not born in December, because shepherds were not keeping their flock in the field in the dead of winter* (Clarke's Commentary, Volume V, p. 370)."

Christmas was known to have been celebrated in Rome in the second quarter of the first century. It was introduced in Antioch about the year 380 in Alexandria. Christmas is really, an Antichrist Mass or mess. When church officials were selecting a day for the celebration of Christmas, they chose December 25 to coincide with Saturn's festival for the sun god (Saturnalia).

Holly's thorns supposedly symbolized the thorns in Christ's crown, and its red berries represented Christ's blood. Holly-Prickly leaves are thorns that were cursed in Genesis 3:18. Even the hanging and decorating of a Christmas tree is not of God and forbidden by the prophet Jeremiah. He says, 3." *For the customs of the people are vain: for one cutteth a tree out of the forest, the work of the hands of the workman with the axe. 4. Thy deck it with silver and gold; they fasten it with nails and hammers, that it move not."-Jeremiah 10:3,4*

The use of evergreen trees, wreaths, and garlands to symbolize eternal life was a custom of the ancient Egyptians, Chinese, and Hebrews. Tree worship was common among the Pagan Europeans and survived their conversion to Christianity. The Christians took over many pagan ideas and images. From sun worship for example, came the celebration of Christ birth on December 25th (I believe Jesus was born during the Feast of Tabernacles in the month of September on around the 29th).

That's why Sun-day is for worship of the sun god. It is not the Sabbath. By changing the sabbath, you set the stage for presenting another Jesus. In A.D. 363 a canon of a council held in Laodicea was passed, pronouncing the death sentence upon any found keeping the Sabbath. Many true Christians were martyred for keeping this day. Before I talk about Santa I want to talk a little more about the Sabbath and sun- god worship.

I want you to notice the unveiled truth, hidden in plain sight that was written in the Davinci code on pages 232, and 233. It is a bit lengthy, but necessary. *"Historians still marvel at the brilliance with which Constantine converted the sun-worshipping pagans to Christianity. By fusing pagan symbols, dates, and rituals into the growing Christian tradition, he created a kind of hybrid religion that was acceptable to both parties. Langdon said. The vestiges of pagan religion in Christian symbology are undeniable. Egyptian sun disks became the halos of Catholic saints."*

Pictograms of Isis nursing her miraculously conceived son Horus became the blueprint for our modern images of the Virgin Mary nursing Baby Jesus. And virtually all the elements of the Catholic ritual—the miter, the altar, the Doxology ,...........Teabing groaned. "Don't get a symbologist started on Christian icons. Nothing in Christianity is original. The pre-Christian god Mithras— called the Son of God and the Light of the World—was born on December 25, died, and was buried in a rock tomb, and then resurrected in three days. By the way, December 25 is also the birthday of Osiris, Adonis, and Dionysus. The newborn Krishna was presented with gold, frankincense, and myrrh. Even Christianity's weekly holy day was stolen from the pagans." "What do you mean?"

"Originally," Langdon said, "Christianity honored the Jewish Sabbath of Saturday, but Constantine shifted it to coincide with the pagan's veneration day of the sun." He paused, grinning. "To this day, most churchgoers attend services on Sunday morning with no idea that they are there on account of the pagan sun god's weekly tribute— Sunday'" (The Da Vinci Code, pp. 232–233)

So, when Constantine emerged as the next emperor he sought for a way to unite his empire. There were only two strong religions, Mithraism, the worship of the sun, and Christianity. Constantine wrote: *"Let all judges and towns-people and occupations of all trades rest on the VENERABLE DAY OF THE SUN. A day of rest. A legal Holiday. . March 7,321 AD. "And upon the day called the day of the sun, all that live ...meet together at the same place where the writings of the apostles and prophets are read. . . "*

The evidence is overwhelming and blatant concerning the Sabbath change. There was even a calendar adjustment, but it never changed the day of the Sabbath as Saturday. God should be worshipped every day. But the Sabbath is holy. The calendar now in use, is a Roman calendar, and has been changed, but the change did not break the weekly cycle. Prior to its change, it was called the Julian calendar, because it originated at the time of Julius Caesar, 45 B.C. Several decades before the birth of Christ. Pope Gregory ordered the one change, and since then it has been known as the Gregorian calendar. The order of days in the week has never been interrupted. Therefore, Saturday remains as the seventh day of the week.

The definition of the word Sabbath is rest, intermission, blessing, refreshing, and holy. It is an intimate scheduled weekly appointment set aside by The Lord Himself, just for you and Him. I want to share some scriptures with you that highlight the importance of the Sabbath, concerning the true Jesus.

"And God blessed the <u>seventh day</u> and sanctified it.: because in it he had <u>rested</u> from all his work, which God created and made."-Genesis 2:27. And he said unto them, "The <u>Sabbath</u> was made for man, and not man for <u>Sabbath</u>: 28. Therefore the Son of man is Lord also of the <u>Sabbath</u>. "- Mark 2:27,28. It is a <u>perpetual</u> (concealed, secret, vanishing point, eternity) covenant between the

*father and His people. (spiritual Israelites -Abraham's
seed) -Exodus 31:13-1716. And He came to Nazareth,
where he had been brought up: and as His custom was, He
went into the synagogue on the <u>Sabbath</u> day, and stood up
for to read." - Luke 4:16*

*14. "But when they departed from Perga, they came
to Antioch in Pisidia, and went into the synagogue on the
<u>Sabbath</u> day, and sat down. 15. And after the reading of the
law and the prophets, the rulers of the synagogue sent unto
them saying, "Ye men and brethren, if ye have any word of
exhortation for the people say on." 42. And when the Jews
were gone out of the synagogue, the gentiles besought that
these words might be preached to them the next <u>Sabbath</u>.
44. And the next <u>Sabbath</u> day came almost the whole city
together to hear the word of God." - Acts 13:14,15 ,42,44.
2. And Paul as his manner was went in unto them, and three
<u>Sabbath</u> days reasoned with them out of the scriptures.
- Acts 17:24. And he reasoned in the synagogue every
<u>Sabbath</u> and persuaded the Jews and the Greeks. - Acts
18:4.*

Moses gives a direct command from the Lord in
Deuteronomy 4:19, about not worshipping the sun. "19.
*"And lest thou lift up thine eyes unto heaven, and when thou
seest the sun, and the moon, and the stars, even all the host
of heaven, shouldest be driven to worship them, and serve
them, which the Lord thy God hath divide unto all nations
under the whole heaven."* God is to be worshipped, <u>not</u>
His creation.

Constantine preached another gospel and preached
another Jesus. Satan has always been about sun worship.
Even with the lie about Easter sunrise service. Easter is
worship of the goddess Ishtar (pronounced Easter). Easter

was originally the celebration of Ishtar, the Assyrian and Babylonian goddess of fertility and sex. The bunnies and eggs represent fertility and birth and child sacrifice and are considered Ishtar's symbols. Easter was celebrated by sacrificing three-month-old babies on an altar at sunrise service on "Easter Sunday," and dying eggs red in the blood. After Constantine decided to Christianize the Empire, Easter was changed to represent Jesus. Or did you really believe eggs and bunnies had anything to do with Jesus' resurrection? Jesus did not rise at sunrise on Easter morning. Jesus rose on the Sabbath, Saturday!

When Mary Magdalene came to the tomb, Sunday morning He was already risen. *20. The first day of the week (Sabbath) cometh Mary Magdalene early, when it was yet dark, unto the sepulchre, and seeth the stone taken away from the sepulchre." – (John 20:1)* The first day of the week on every calendar has always been Sunday and the seventh day of the week has always been Saturday. So, who is THIS Jesus that the whole world worships on Ishtar (Easter), Sunday, and Christmas, Mithras birthday? Not the Jesus of Nazareth. The sun god is always connected with a woman. The Semiramis and Nimrod syndrome has been used by Satan throughout the history of humankind to mimic Jesus and his life.

In China, Shing Moo is the Holy Mother. In India Devaki is the goddess, and Crishna is the child. In Greece Aphrodite is the goddess. In Ephesus Diana is the holy goddess. In Egypt Isis is the goddess, and Horus is the child. In Rome, Venus is the goddess, Cupid is the child. In Israel Ashteroth is the goddess, Baal is the child. It all stems from Babylon, (confusion, Cain's town), different forms of Semiramis and Tammuz (Baal). When Ezekiel was shown this, he was able to feel the disappointment the Lord had in the actions of sun god worship.

14. *" Then he brought me to the door of the gate of the Lord's house which was toward the North; and, behold, there sat women weeping for Tammuz (Sun god, Nimrod). 15.Then he said unto me, Hast thou seen this, O son of man? turn thee yet again and thou shalt see greater abominations than these. 16And he brought me into the inner court of the Lord's house, and, behold at the temple of the Lord, between the porch and the altar...their faces toward the east and they worshipped the sun toward the east. "* -Ezekiel 8:14-16.

Nimrod is Tammuz, son of Semiramis and claims to be Baal reincarnated. Tammuz is a false Christ masquerading as another Jesus. This is exactly how Satan masquerades as Santa during Christmas time. He pretends to be just like Jesus.

If you rearrange the letters in the word *"Santa"* you get *"Satan."* The reason is because they are the same. According to legend, Santa began as a 4th century catholic Bishop named St. Nicholas which was shortened to *"Sinter Klaus* (Later Santa Claus)." St. Nicholas day was never on December 25th. Traits of Santa borrowed from Thor. Santa Claus is not the Bishop St. Nicholas but his dark helper. The Christian Demon Knecht Rupprecht was a companion of St. Nicholas in a play in 1668 and was condemned by the Roman Catholic for being a devil in 1680. Thomas Nast drew the first Santa as a fur clad, small troll like figure. Santa and Satan are altering egos. Opposites on the surface but the same underneath. I will list some scriptures below to display how Santa (Satan) is portraying another Jesus.

".... And thou shalt call his name..." – Matthew 1:21. The name Santa Claus is like Satan's claws. Kris Kringle is German for little Christ child. *"His head and his hairs were white like wool, as white as snow..." – Revelation 1:14. 'Who is this that cometh.... red in thine apparel." – Isaiah 63:2. "And his feet...... as if they burned in a furnace."- Revelation 1:15. "Verily, Verily, I say unto you, he that entereth not by the door into the sheepfold, but climbeth up some other way, the same is a thief and a robber." – John 10;1.* Santa enters by chimney. *"Is not this the carpenter......" – Mark 6:3.*

"His house.... was toward the North.' – Ezekiel 8:14. Everyone knows Santa lives at the *North Pole. "And they clothed him with purple and platted a crown of thorns and put it about his head." – Mark 15:17.* To many this Holly wreath represents the crown of thorns that Jesus wears and the red berries symbolize his blood that he shed. *"... who rideth upon the heaven in thy help......" – Deut.32:26.* Santa rides in the heavens on his reindeer. *"Ho, ho...saith the Lord...." –* Zechariah 2:6. Doesn't Santa say, *"Ho, Ho, Ho?" "...and his angels were cast out with him.' – Revelation 12:9.* An Elf is a wandering spirit, an evil spirit and a devil. *"...for his great love where with he loved us.' – Ephesians 2:4. "...Ask, and it shall be given you ..." – Matthew 7:7. "All power is given to me in Heaven and in Earth.* He is all knowing, all powerful, and he is everywhere.

The Christmas Spirit is an evil, magical, spirit of deception. *"I will pour out my spirit..." – Proverbs 1:23. "... then he shall sit upon the throne of his glory." – Matthew 25:31. "...were judged out of those things written in books, according to their works.' – Revelation*

20:12. Only the genuine Jesus of Nazareth, The Son of The Living God, knows when we are sleeping. And knows when we are awake. Jesus knows if we've been bad or good. Santa, Christmas, and the Christmas spirit is the spirit of antichrist in disguise.

Another Spirit:

There is *another spirit* in the world today and it attempts to emulate The Holy Ghost. The antichrist spirit takes the place of the Holy Spirit. According to *1 John 4:3, "3. And every spirit that confesseth not that Jesus Christ is come in the flesh is not of God: and this is that spirit of antichrist, whereof ye heard that it should come; and even now it is already in the world."*

There is an evil spirit by the name of *Kundalini* which has its origin the Garden of Eden. *Kundalini* is a New Age spirit known as *"The coiled one with serpent power."* Kundalini operates as primal energy released through chakras through the base of the spine. It is through deep meditation, mantras, breathing, and chanting, and the foundation of Yoga. It copies the manifestations of the Holy Ghost. Many of today's preachers operate through and release this Kundalini spirit on their congregations, because they are deceived. It is directly connected with their oath and union with Freemasons and Lucifer.

Kundalini will mimic the Holy Spirit in a myriad of ways. Some instances are false tongues, feeling false fire, false heat, false wind, being slain in the spirit by a false spirit, false prophesying, false healings, and excessive false laughter.

The only way to accurately mimic something is to look and act exactly like it. One of the key ways to notice this is if the person seems like the Kundalini spirit is controlling them spirit beyond one's will. The Holy Ghost will never violate your will and make you do something without your permission, request, and cooperation. Kundalini takes control of the person. Kundalini puts you under a transcendental spell and in a demonic trance, an awakens the spiritual being. That's why John tells us, *"Beloved, believe not every spirit, but try the spirits whether they are of God: because many false prophets are gone out into the world (1 John 4:1)."*

Kundalini is associated with and resembles The Nehutsan, Moses' serpent of brass. But the people started to worship it and see it as God. Something that appeared to be holy had become a curse. In 2 Kings 18:4, Joshua broke it in pieces and destroyed it. The genuine Holy Ghost will bear true witness within your redeemed spirit and confirm everything by the true word of God, and not *another gospel.*

Another Gospel:

It does not matter how rich, famous, successful, and anointed a preacher may appear to be, if he or she preaches any other gospel than the true gospel, he or she must be rejected. We must inspect the fruit, and even squeeze it sometimes. The word tells us in Galatians 1:6-9, *"6. I marvel that you are so soon removed from him that called you into the grace of Christ unto another gospel. 7. Which is not another; but there may be some that trouble you and would pervert the gospel of Christ. 8. But though we, or an angel from heaven, preach any other gospel unto you than that which we have preached unto you, let him be accursed. 9. as we said before, so I say now again, if any man preach another gospel than that ye have received let him be accursed."*

Wow! Even if an angel from heaven preaches another gospel. That is why they are fallen angels from the heavenly realms. Many false religions were started because a person received a visitation from an angel of God. But the problem was that the angel or spirit being preached unto them something contrary to the word. An angel of God would never contradict the Word of God!

There was a sect of believers in the days of the Apostles who would contradict them and bring confusion through *another gospel.* It was a false system of teachings that existed during early centuries of Christianity. These men were known as *Gnostics*, and they practiced *Gnosticism,* which means knowledge. They believed that God was bad, and Satan was good. They believe that the tree of knowledge represents spiritual freedom that God was supposedly trying to keep from man. Gnostics would go behind the disciples and pervert the gospel of the kingdom.

Gnostics believed that knowledge was the way to salvation, not The Lord Jesus. That one must be enlightened and initiated through a spiritual awakening *(Kundalini)*, or knowledge of self. They believed that a person had the freedom to participate in all sorts of indulgences, and that it doesn't matter how you live. This sounds like That Old Nacash's dialogue in the Garden of Eden. Doesn't it sound like today's gospel of many Freemason, Illuminati preachers. These preachers are controlled and censored by their Church's tax-exempt status through the 501C3. The

501C3 makes the Pastors associated with it, preach *another gospel.* Unfortunately, these pastors know that abandoning the 501C3, would mean losing benefits, privileges, access, political ties and most importantly, money. It is essentially a contract of marriage with Baal.

The 501C3 takes away the church's rights and makes them the property of the government, making the church an artificial person. The pastor's freedom of speech is taken away. When this occurs, the pastor is censored and begins preaching *another gospel.* 501C3 forbids speaking against abortion, LGBTQ, Illuminati, New World Order, Freemasons, politicians, and political candidates.

Prior to 1954, churches were free to evaluate the positions of political candidates on moral issues without fear of the internal revenue service revoking their tax-exempt status. That year, then Senator Lyndon Johnson amended the tax code to add the threat of IRS action against churches if those pastors mentioned specific candidates from the pulpit. There is other tax-exempt contracts that can be used that does not seek to control the messenger. 501C3 is ran by the Illuminati in conjunction with the Freemason entities, CIA, FBI, DEA, and the IRS (usually they have 3 letters).

The 501C3 removes a church's and their congregation's constitutional rights. When you sign the 501C3 contract, you willingly gave the IRS legal power to tell your church what messages it can and cannot preach. The 501C3 promotes preaching freedom and grace and not sin and judgement.

You'll hear them say, *"Once saved, always saved."* They say, *"we are not under the law, but under grace."* The biggest lie of all is, *"The Holy Spirit won't convict you of sin."* God is merciful to forgive true repentance, but we are to strive to live holy and not rely on grace as a crutch, the implication is that we are free to break the ten commandments. We are commanded to endure until the end. When the truth is that we should be working out our salvation, daily, with fear and trembling.

The truth is that we are to strive to live sin free and holy and endure until the end. Don't rely on another gospel of greasy grace, because sin has consequences! Salvation does not come through knowledge. It only comes one way, and that is through a person. He was crucified on the cross, buried in a tomb, resurrected in glory, and is alive today. His name is Jesus The Christ of Nazareth. He is the Son of God! He is God! He is the only way to the Father and everlasting salvation. Through salvation The Father will use The Holy Ghost to open our eyes and unveil the truth Of Our Lord and King Jesus.

The word *revelation* means to unveil or take off the cover. The Lord has unveiled the truth in this book about the many secrets of the world of Satan. These truths have been hidden in the Bible in plain sight. Now you know the truth about what happened in the Garden of Eden. Everything that went on then is happening now. Those same beings, fallen angels, that roamed the Garden of Eden are roaming the earth now as disguised impostors, working for Nacash. But now your eyes are opened! Do your own research and ask the Holy Spirit about the truth in this book.

In conclusion, I thank Jesus for the revelation and that He has a President in the White House that is ready to *TRUMP* all of the *OBAMANATIONS* in America, and unveil the secrets, for a true cleansing of this Country. It's already started. There is a movement called #METOO. In this movement droves of Hollywood stars are coming out and revealing that they were raped, or sexually harassed. I guess that sex spell WAS effective. But the Living Word of God is much, much more EFFECTIVE and UNDEFEATED! When someone tells you a secret, you can't wait to tell it. And people can't wait to hear it. Well, The secret is out and has been unveiled.

I also want to thank The Heavenly Father in advance, by faith for eradicating the document of the Official Witch of Los Angeles County, and breaking the spell off Los Angeles, Hollywood, and the whole world!

Prophetic Decree:

Therefore, I make a decree that every people, nation, and language speak not anything against the God of Shadrach, Meshach and Abednego, because there is no God that can deliver of this sort. I make a decree that in every dominion of the (city, nation, continent) men and women tremble before the name of Jesus who is the God of the Bible. For He is the living God, and steadfast forever, and His kingdom is that which shall not be destroyed. His dominion shall be even unto the end. He delivers and rescues and He works signs, wonders, and miracles in Heaven and on Earth. He shall overturn, overthrow, and overcome the secret powers behind the secret societies, and pour out His spirit upon an awakened repentant people. May the King of Glory rule and reign. The Lord strong and Almighty in Battle.

Prayer for your City, County, Nation: Revival- Outpouring-

Gracious Heavenly Father,

Bless you Lord. You are the Lord God of Israel and America *(your country)*. You only do wondrous things! Bless you Lord for you have shown your marvelous kindness in this strong city. Let your hand be heavy here. Let there be repentance, deliverance, healing, and great joy in this city of Los Angeles *(your city)*. …….. O Lord, according to all thy righteousness, I beseech thee let thine anger and thy fury be turned away from thy city as we repent. We repent for our sins, and the iniquities of our fathers. Los Angeles (Insert Your City), and thy people are become a reproach to all that are about us.

Now therefore, O, our God, incline thine ear and hear; open thine eyes, and behold our desolations, and the city which is called by thy name: for we do not present our supplications before thee, not for our righteousness, but for your great mercies.

O Lord, hear; O Lord, forgive; O Lord hearken and do; defer not for thine own sake, O my God: for thy city of Los Angeles *(your city)* and thy people are called by thy name.

O Lord we repent of the sex spell, fornication, pornography, pedophilia, molestations, rapes, and bestiality committed in this city. We repent of the love of mammon, gangs, racism, abortions, homosexuality, the LGBTQP agenda, gay marriage, adultery, lies, and false god worship. We repent of the ritual human sacrifices committed in our territory.

Forgive us for the allowing the multitude of whoredoms, sorceries, witchcrafts, necromancy, casting spells, charmers, shamans, enchantments, incantations, operation of witches, wizards, and warlocks, in Los Angeles (*your city*). Forgive us not putting you first. We are sorry, Lord. We repent.

Let the presence and glory of the Lord be present in L.A. (*your city*). Cleanse this city, county, and state. Loose your Cherubim to scatter coals of repentance on this city. Loose your Seraphim to baptize this city with fire. This city of Los Angeles is no longer the caldron and we are no longer the meat or the flesh. Our children, and youth belong to you, Lord. Let the spirit of repentance fall on this city. Let the name of Los Angeles (*your city*) be, "The Lord is There." Los Angeles (*your city*) will be a city sought out, and not forsaken.

Lord expose, reject and eject ancient territorial spirits that have been in secret, hiding in Los Angeles (*your city*). Release demons of pride, tradition, ego, lust, and religion. Unstop, unclog, and cleanse the portal over this city. Choose this city to rest your presence, and power. Release love, miracles, signs, wonders, and healings to an unprecedented level. Have mercy on us O Lord. Pour out your spirit, blood, fire, and glory on Los Angeles (your city). Let revival start and spread like a wild forest fire in this city, in Jesus name!

About The Author

Dr. Etienne M. Graves Jr. is prophet and founder of MEMO Ministries (Melchizedek's Excellent Ministry Order), located in Los Angeles and the Inland Empire in California. He is a prophetic messenger who travels the World and is available for speaking engagements.

Etienne uses visual aids to deliver God's message and reveal the hidden secrets in God's word. As a chosen vessel of the Lord his calling is to be used as God's secret weapon to attack the enemy with the uncompromising truth of the Word of God. Dr. Graves shares the unprecedented revelation about the garden of Eden, Angels, Satan, DNA, the Order of Melchizedek, and Nephilim.

He has been anointed and used by the Holy Ghost in the gifts of healing. Etienne is the author of, "Demons Nephilim Angels: The World That Then Was." Etienne was the featured speaker on Angelic Incursion at the 2016 Nephcon conference in Texas.

Dr. Graves received a Doctor of Divinity and humane letters Degree in June 2017 from Victory in Praise University.

WORKS CITED

1.   Graves Jr, Etienne M. *Demons Nephilim Angels: The World That Then Was*. Los Angeles: Trafford Publishing, 2014.

2.   Watson, James D.,*The Double Helix: A Personal account of the discovery of the structure of DNA*. New York: Scribner Publishing, 1968.

3.   Charles, R. H. *The Book of Enoch*. Eugene: Wipf & Stock Publishers, 2005.

4.   Horn, Thomas. *Nephilim Stargates: The Year 2012 and the Return of the Watchers. Crane*: Anomalos Publishing House, 2007.

5.   Horn, Thomas and Chris D. Putnam. *Exo- Vaticana. Crane: Defender,* 2013

6.   Kirban, Salem. *Satan's Angels Exposed*. Rossville: Grapevine Book Distributors, 1980.

7.   Malone, Henry. *Portals To Cleansing*. Irving: Vision Life Publication, 2002.

8.   Cooper, William Milton. *Behold A Pale Horse*. Flagstaff: Light Technology Publications, 1991.

9.   Bramley, William. *The Gods of Eden*. New York: Harper Collins Publishers, 1989.

10.   Hall, P. Manly. *The Secret Teachings of All Ages*. San Francisco: H.S. Crocker Company Inc, 1928.

11.   Hall, Manly P. *Rosicrucians and Masonic Origins*. Los Angeles: hall Publishing Compnay, 1st ed, 1929.

12.   Ronayne, Edmond. *The Master's Carpet or Masonry and Baal-Worship Identical*: (Reviewing the similarity between Masonry, Romanism and "The Mysteries," and comparing the whole with the Bible). Chicago: T.B. Arnold, 1887.

13.   Finney, Charles G., *The Character, Claims and Practical Workings of Freemasonry*. National Christian Association, 1948(1869).

14.   Brown, Dan. T*he Da Vinci Code*. (US) Doubleday, Transworld and Bantam Books, 2003.

15.   Flemming, Rev. John. *The Fallen Angels and the Heroes of the Myth*. Dublin: Hodges, Foster, and Figgis, 1879.

16.   Simon. Papal Magic: *Occult Practices Within the Catholic Church*. New York: HarperCollins Publishers Inc. – https://www.harpercollinsebooks.com.

17.   Jastrow, Morris. *The Religion of Babylonia and Assyria*. Bibliolife, 2009.

18.   Hislop, Alexander. *The Tale of Two Babylons.* (Pdf. Adobe Reader). Presbyterian Free Church of Scotland, 1853.

19.   Klosterman, Chuck, *I Wear the Black Hat.* Scribner Publishing, New York, 2013.

20.   Gabler, Neal. *An Empire of Their Own: How the Jews Invented Hollywood.* Anchor Books, New York, 1988.

21.   Strong, James. T*he New Strong's Exhaustive Concordance of the Bible.* Nashville: Thomas Nelson Publishers, 2010.

22.   Lockyer Sr, Herbert., Bruce, F.F., Harison, R.K., *Illustrated Dictionary of the Bible.* Nashville: Thomas Nelson Publishers, 1986.

23.   Isbouts, Jean-Pierre. *Secret Societies: True Tales of Covert Cults and Organizations and Their Leaders.* Washington: National Geoghraphic Partners LLC, 2017.

24.   Sinistrari of Ameno, Rev. Father. *Demoniality; or Incubi and Succubi. Original Latin Manuscript.* London: 1872-google books

25.   Select Committee on Intelligence., Subcommittee on Health and Scientific Research., Committee on Human Resources United States Senate. (95th Congress) *Project MKULTRA, The CIA's Program of Research in Behavioral Modification.* Washington: US Government Printing Office, 1977.

26.   Robison, John (Professor of Natural Philosophy and Secretary to the Royal Society of Edinburgh.). *Proofs of a Conspiracy against all the Religions and Governments of Europe, Carried on in the Secret Meetings of Freemasons, Illuminati, and Reading Societies.* New York: George Foreman, No. 64 Water-Street, 1798.

27.   Teichrib, Carl. *The Power Puzzle: A Compilation of Documents and Resources on Global Governance.* World System Research Institute, 2nd ed, 2004.

28.   Tindall, William. *Standard History of the City of Washinton: From A Study of the Original Sources.* Knoxville: H.W. Crew & Co., 1914.

29.   Academy of Medical Sciences, The British Academy, The Royal Academy of Engineering and The Royal Society. *Human Enhancement and the Future of Work.* The Academy of Medical Sciences, November 2012.

30.   *The American Heritage College Dictionary.* 3rd ed. Boston: Houghton Mifflin C0., 1993

31.   *The Companion Bible King James Version.* Grand Rapids: Kregel Publications, 1922.

32.   Rea more: http://www.dailymail.co.uk/news/article-1378184/Woman-discovers-twins-sons-DIFFERENT-fathers-The- Maury-Show.html#ixzz3spDyoSs7

33. Read more: http://www.dailymail.co.uk/news/article-1378184/Woman-discovers-twins-sons-DIFFERENT-fathers-The-Maury-Show.html#ixzz3spDNgYPw.

34. http://www.today.com/parents/working-moms-prioritizing-time-crucial-2D80555028.

35. Huebner, Louise. L.A. *Witches Story, official Witch of Los Angeles.* Website design by Wolfden Creations, 2003. –

36. (http://www.mentorhebnerart.com/witchstuff/officialwitch.shtml).

37. Brown, Rich (1999). *"Lucy Liu's Bizarre Sex Tale."* TV Guide Online. September 14, 1999.

38. (2004). FHM magazine Interview. Anna Nicole Smith (Issue #46) FHM Magazine, emap-metro, July, 2004.

39. (2018). *Time Magazine Special Edition. 1968: The Year That Shaped A Generation,* Times Inc Books, New York, 2018.

40. Spitznagel, Eric. Q & A: Dan Aykroyd on Sleeping with a Ghost, Aliens, Vodka, & Doctor Detroit. Esquire Magazine, 2013.

41. Seacrets, Ryan. Ke$ha: *I had Sex With A Ghost.* KIIS FM Radio Interview, Los Angeles: September 27, 2012.

42.   Shuter, Rob. *"CoCo Austin recalls Encounter With Perverted Ghost."* Huffington Post, "Naughty But Nice," talkshow-HD Net.

43.   (http://www.hufingtonpost.com/2012/03/01/coco-austin-perverted-ghost_n_1313423.html).

44.   Bosquet, Jean. *Lizard Peoples Catacomb City Hunted. Did Strange People Live Under Site of Los Angeles 5000 Years Ago?* L.A.: Los Angeles Times, January 29, 1934.

45.   (http://www.dailymail.co.uk/news/article-1378184/ Woman-discovers-twin-sons-DIFFERENT-fathers-The-Maury-Povich-Show.html).

46.   (https://www.google.com/amp/s/ww.today.com/ amp/parents/mother-gives-birth-twins-different-dads-2D80554133).

47.   Clarke, Adam. *Clarke's Commentary Volume 5.* Abingdon Press, 1966.

48.   Wolfe, David Avocado. *Punctuation Is Powerful: MEME-*

49.   Facebook- 2015

50.   Video- Lost Walt Disney *UFO Documentary- Full Uncut Version*

CPSIA information can be obtained
at www.ICGtesting.com
Printed in the USA
BVHW040044200121
598135BV00010B/332